A LOOK INTO
Chinese Art
Babylonian Art

Conceived, Designed, and Illustrated by:

Mrinal Mitra

Series edited by:

Swarna Mitra & **Malika Mitra**

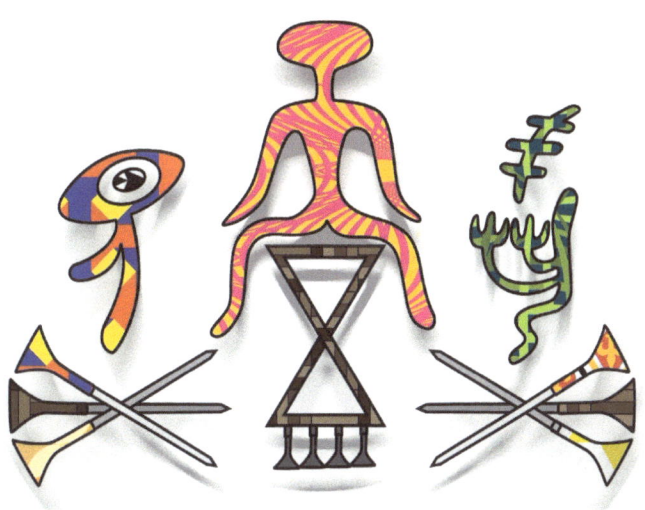

This series is dedicated to the citizens of the world;
from the young blooming minds of children, to the aspired individuals of all ages.

THE WORLD CULTURE ART
VOLUME-5

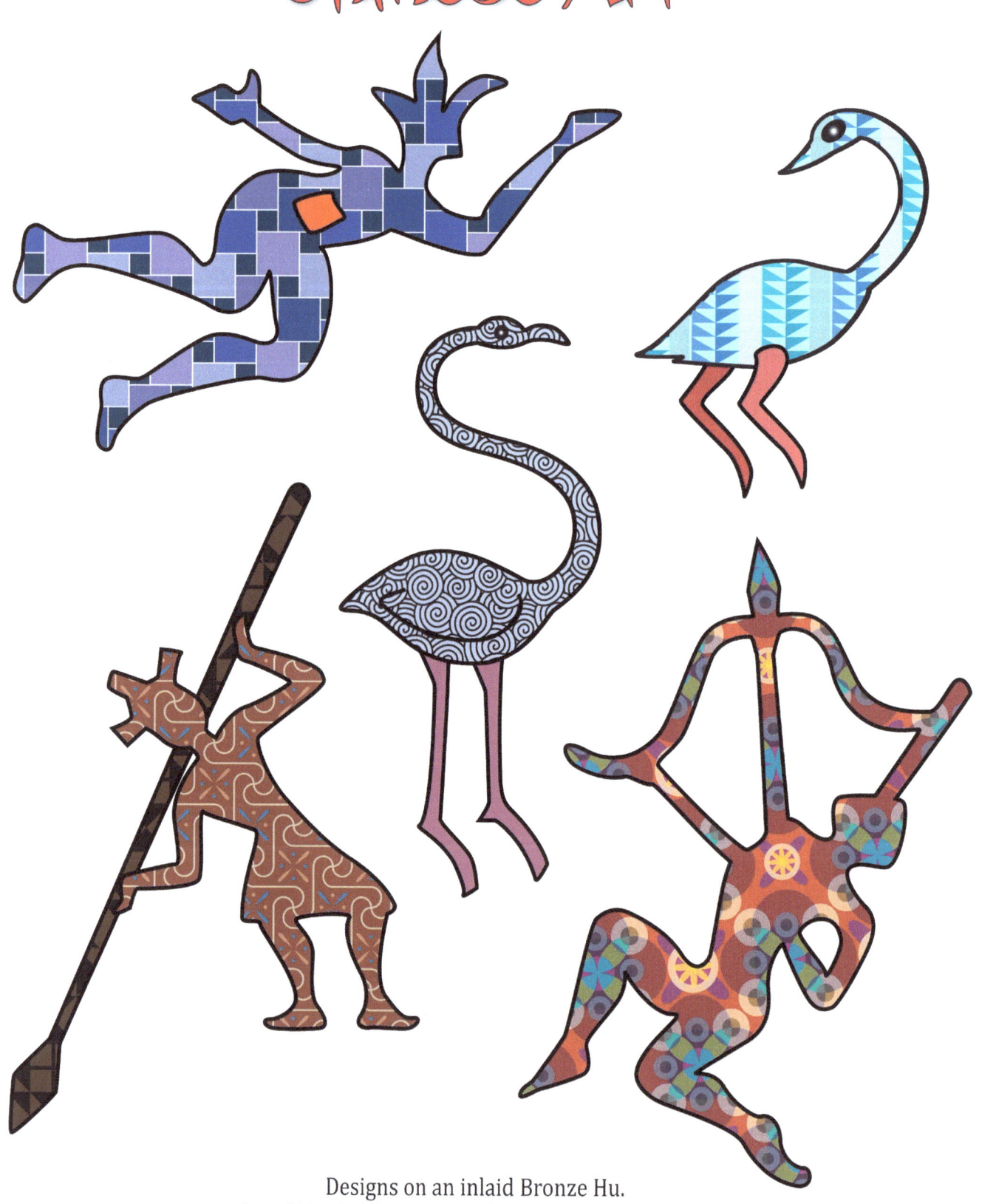

Designs on an inlaid Bronze Hu.
Late Warring States Period. 475 B.C.E. - 221 B.C.E.

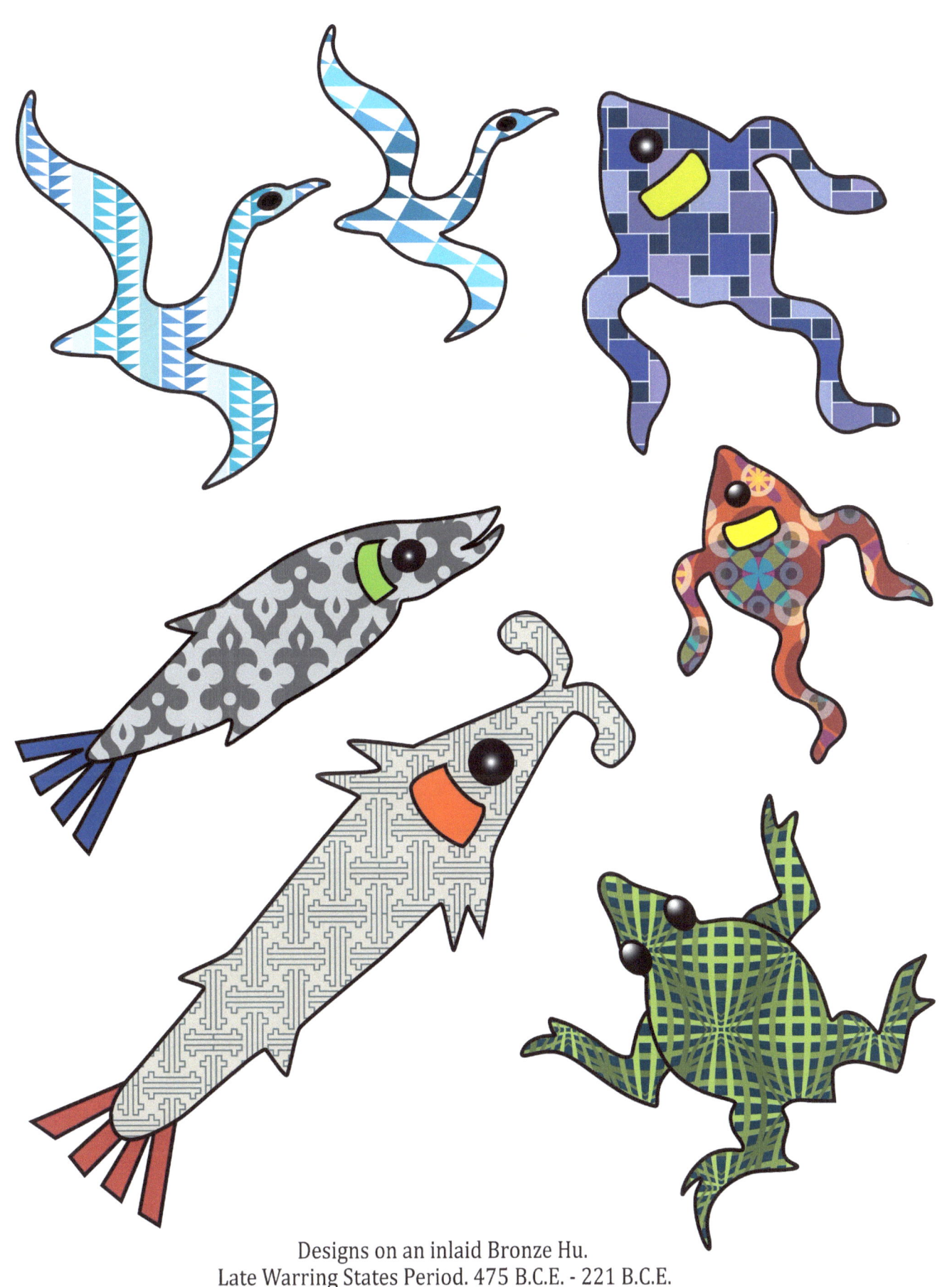

Designs on an inlaid Bronze Hu.
Late Warring States Period. 475 B.C.E. - 221 B.C.E.

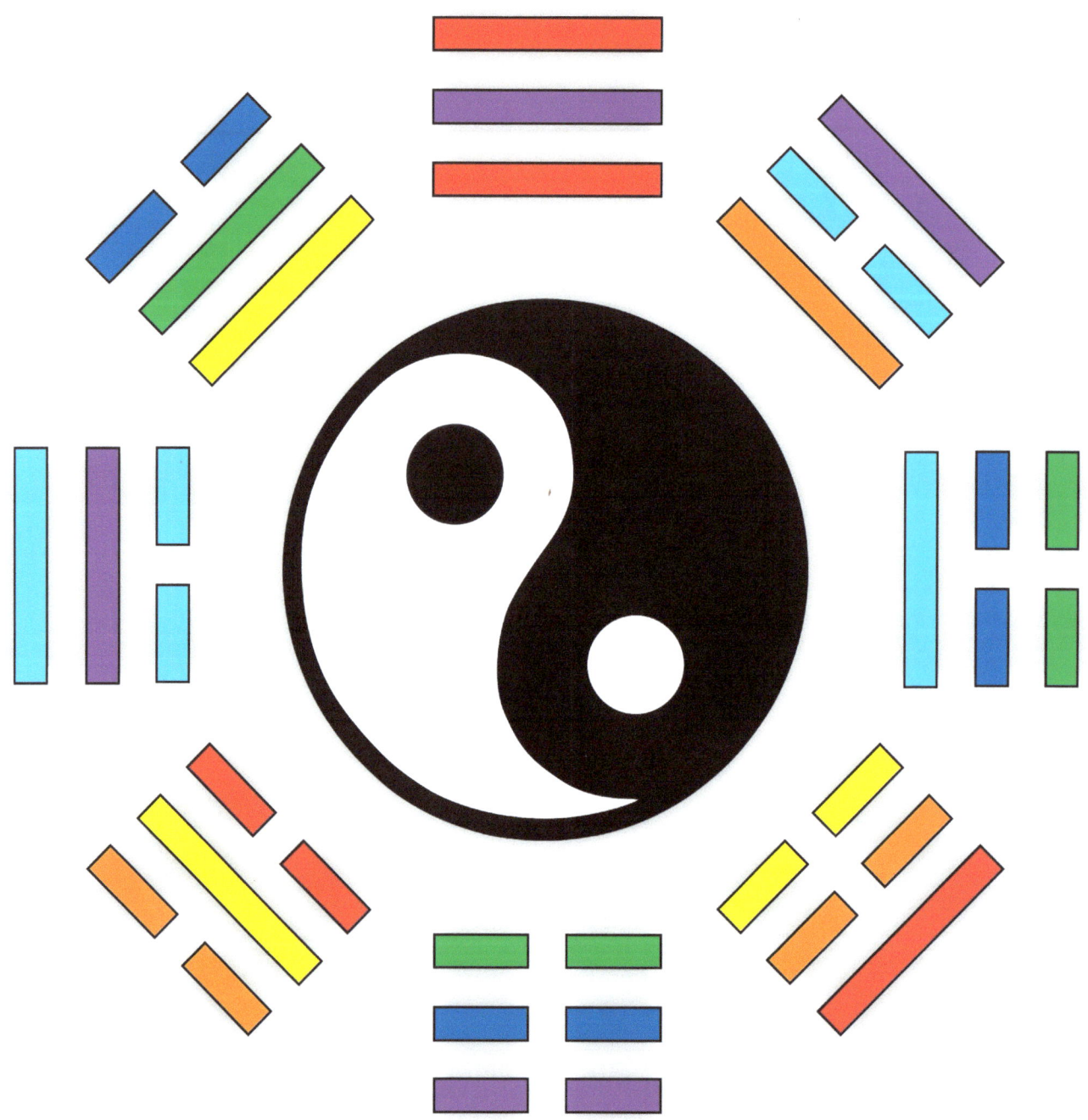

Yin and Yang, Dao Symbol. Daoism called humankind
to follow the natural, cosmic flow of the universe.

Yin and Yang are the prime forces of the universe, surrounded by eight trigrams.
The mystical symbols were viewed as the will of the God. The trigrams are supposedly
discovered by Fu Hsi, the mythical emperor who reigned in 2953 B.C.E.

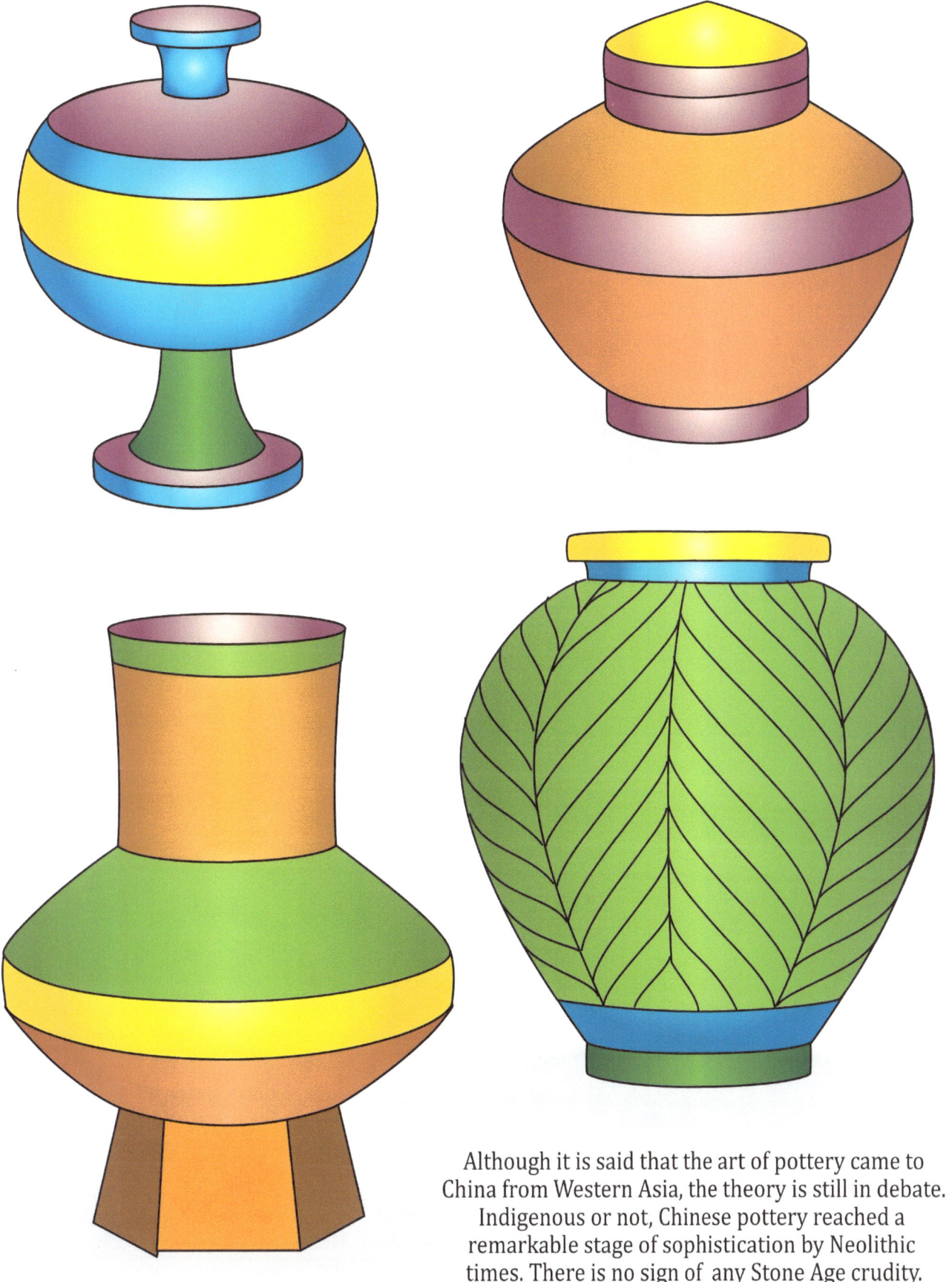

Although it is said that the art of pottery came to
China from Western Asia, the theory is still in debate.
Indigenous or not, Chinese pottery reached a
remarkable stage of sophistication by Neolithic
times. There is no sign of any Stone Age crudity.

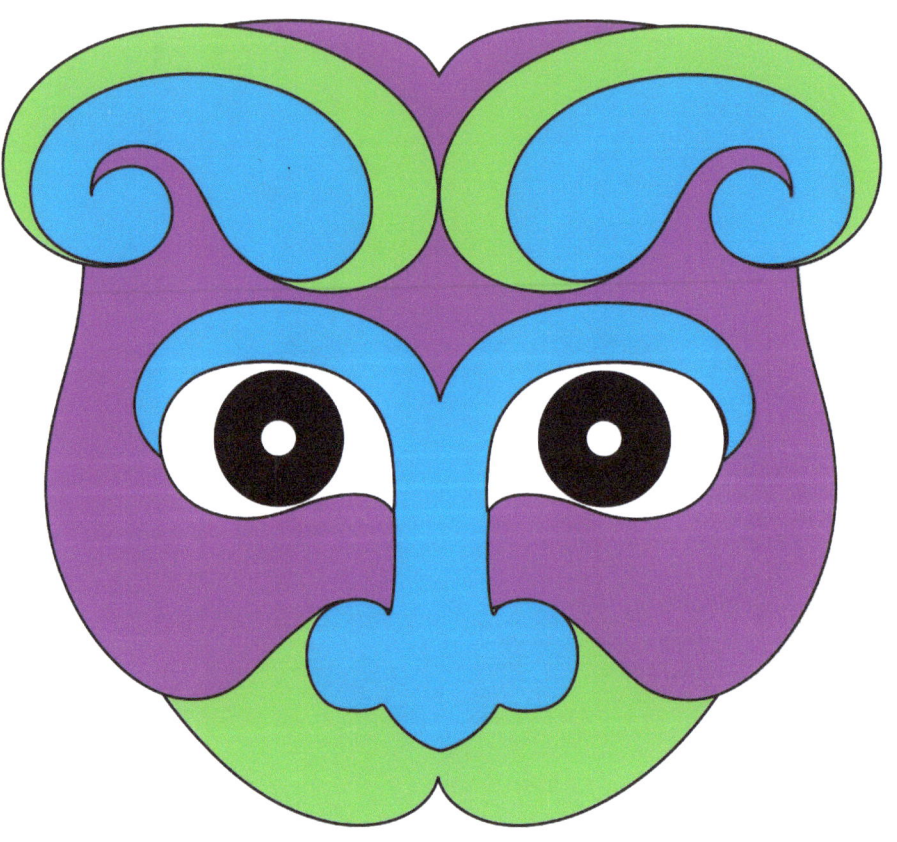

On a vertical bronze vessel.
Shang Dynasty, 1766 B.C.E. - 1121 B.C.E.

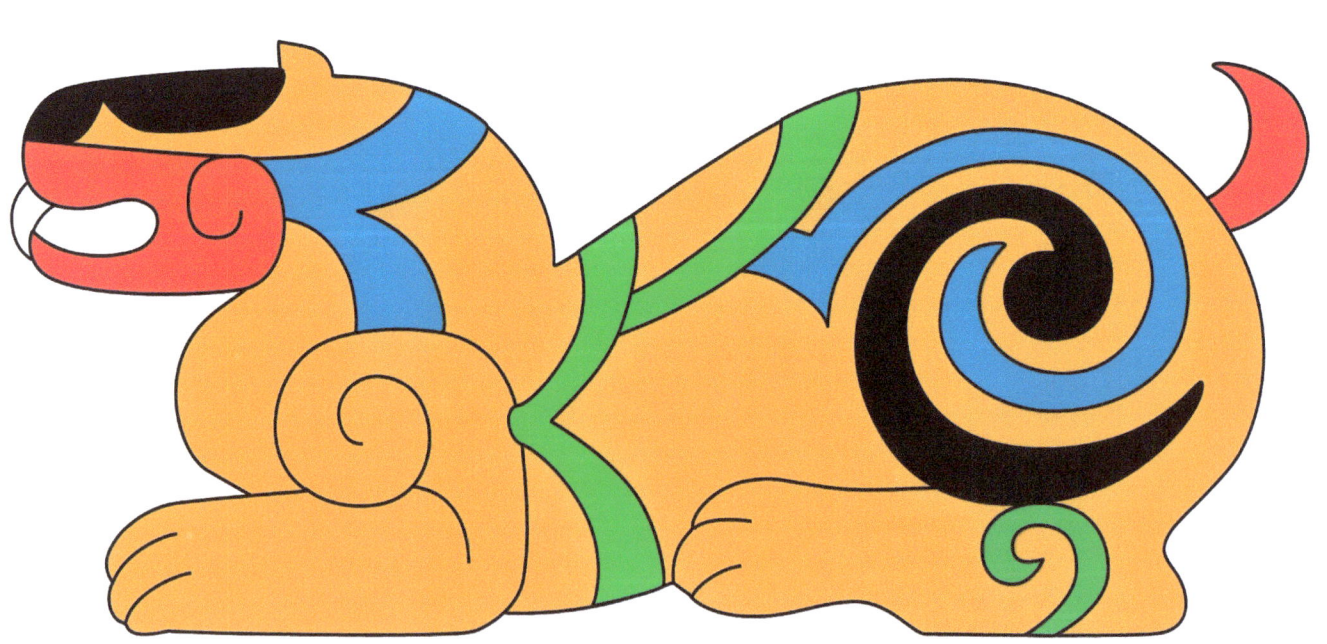

Stylized animal drawing on a
drum or gong stand. Warring States Period, 475 B.C.E. - 221 B.C.E.

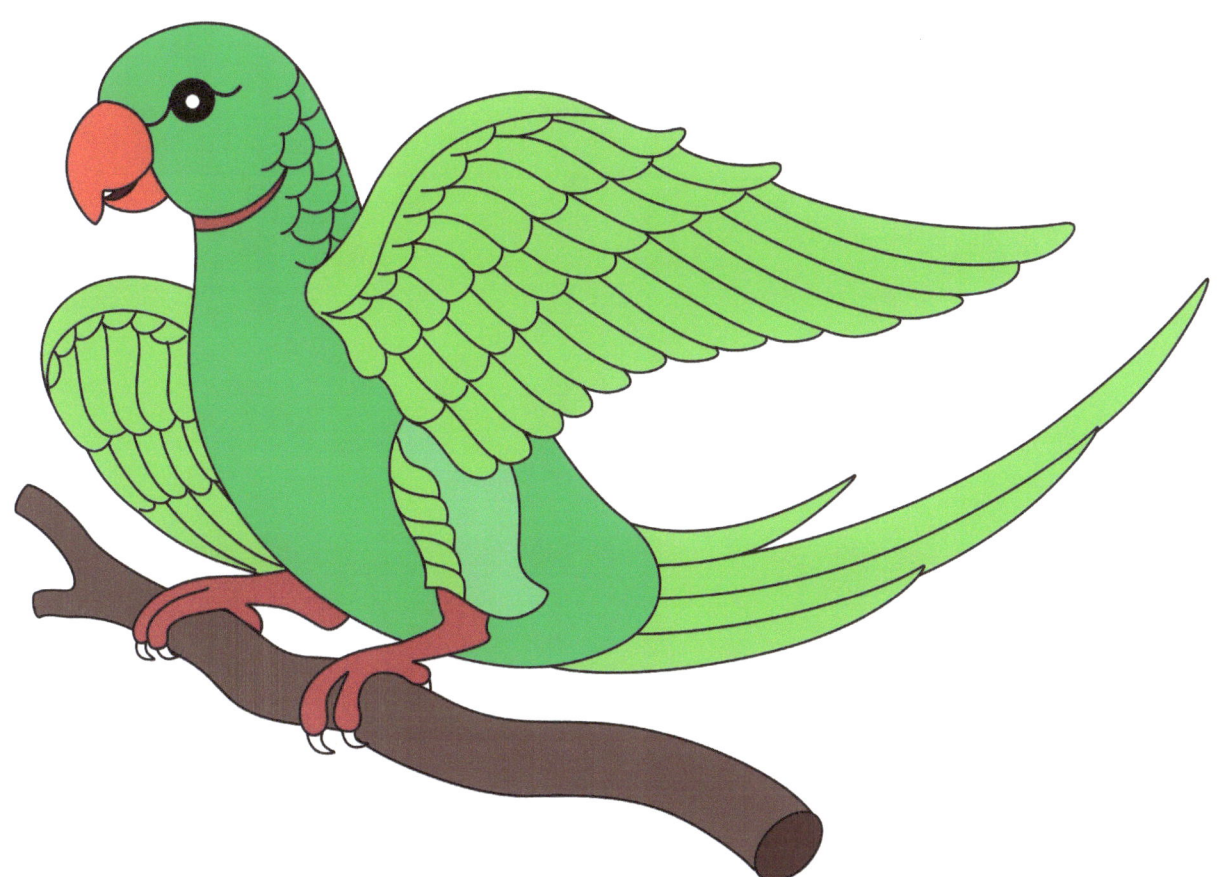

Stylized drawing of a parrot found in a decorated covered jar.
Tang Dynasty, 618 C.E. - 907 C.E.

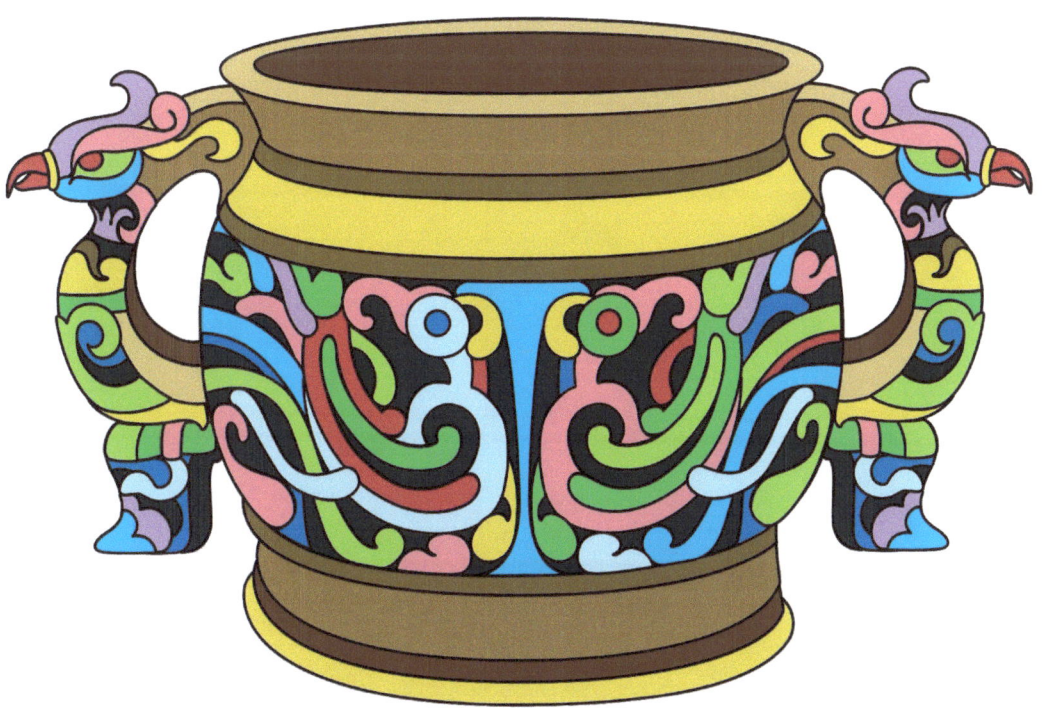

Shang- Zhou Bronze vessel for rituals.

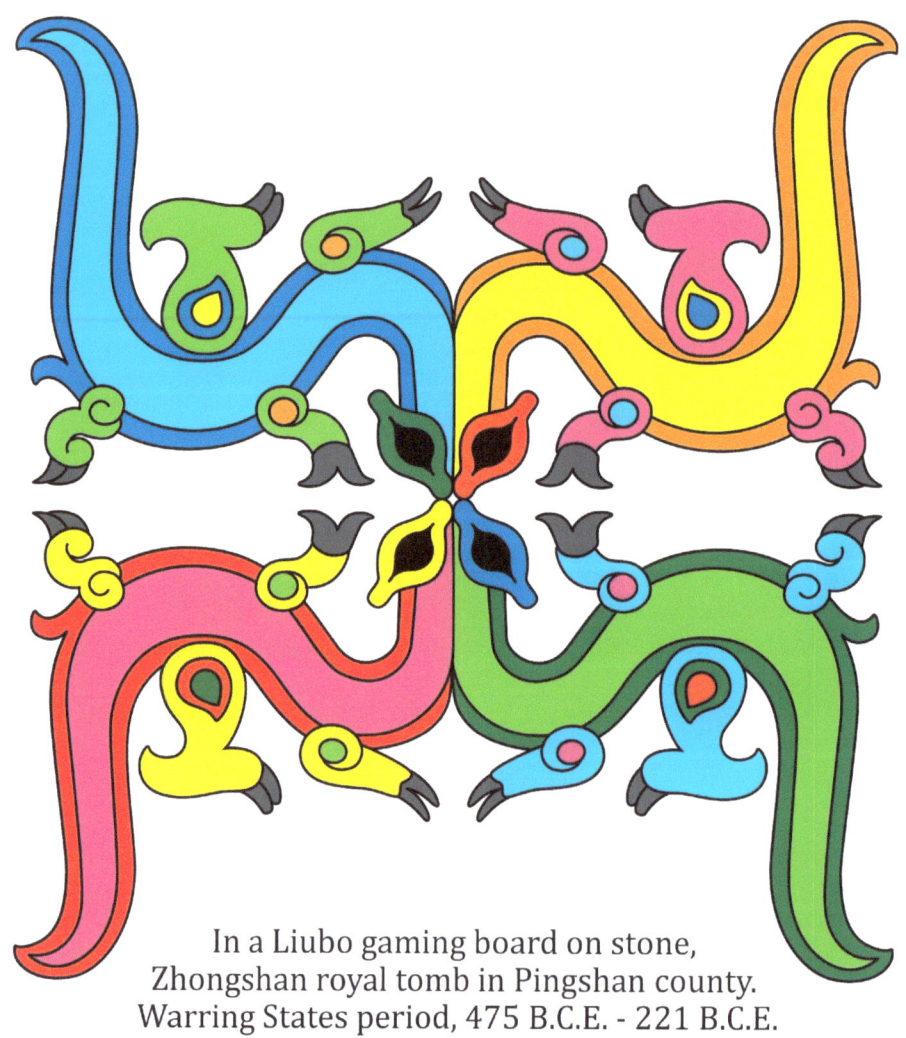

In a Liubo gaming board on stone,
Zhongshan royal tomb in Pingshan county.
Warring States period, 475 B.C.E. - 221 B.C.E.

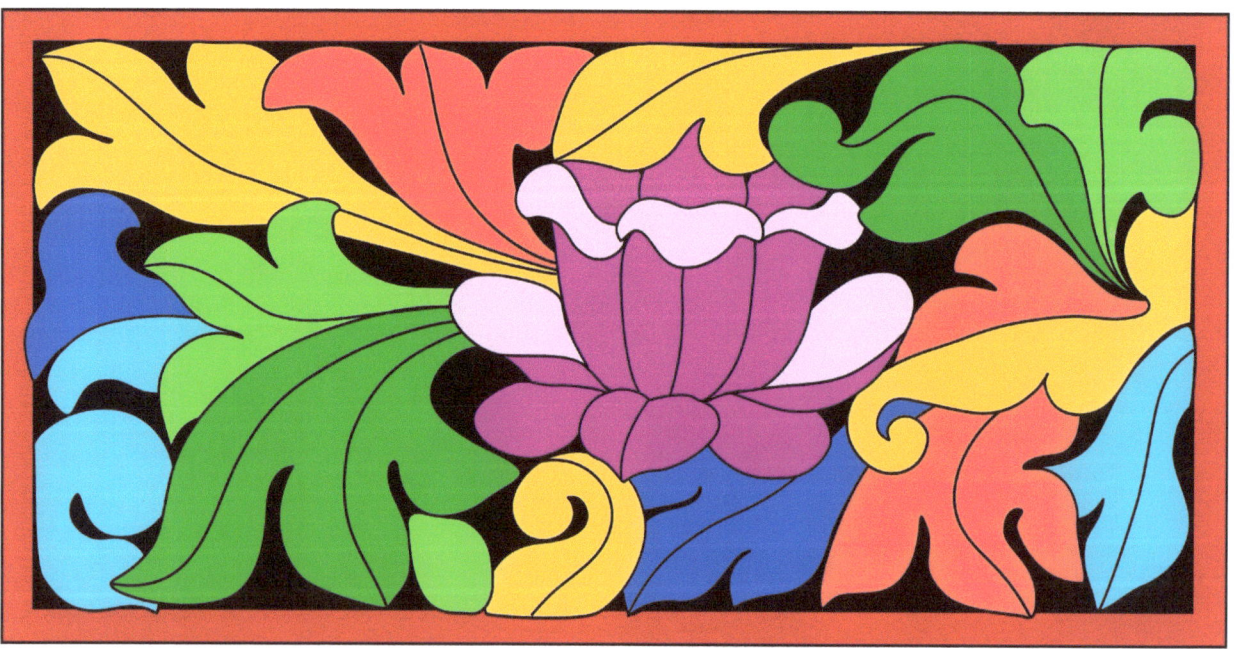

Floral relief work on the wall during Shenzong reign. Circa 1000 B.C.E.

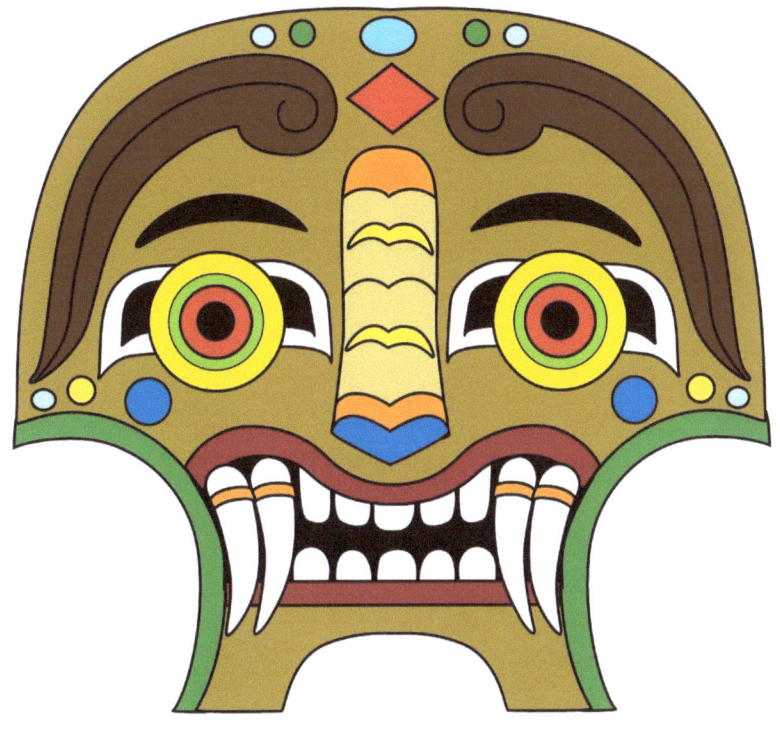

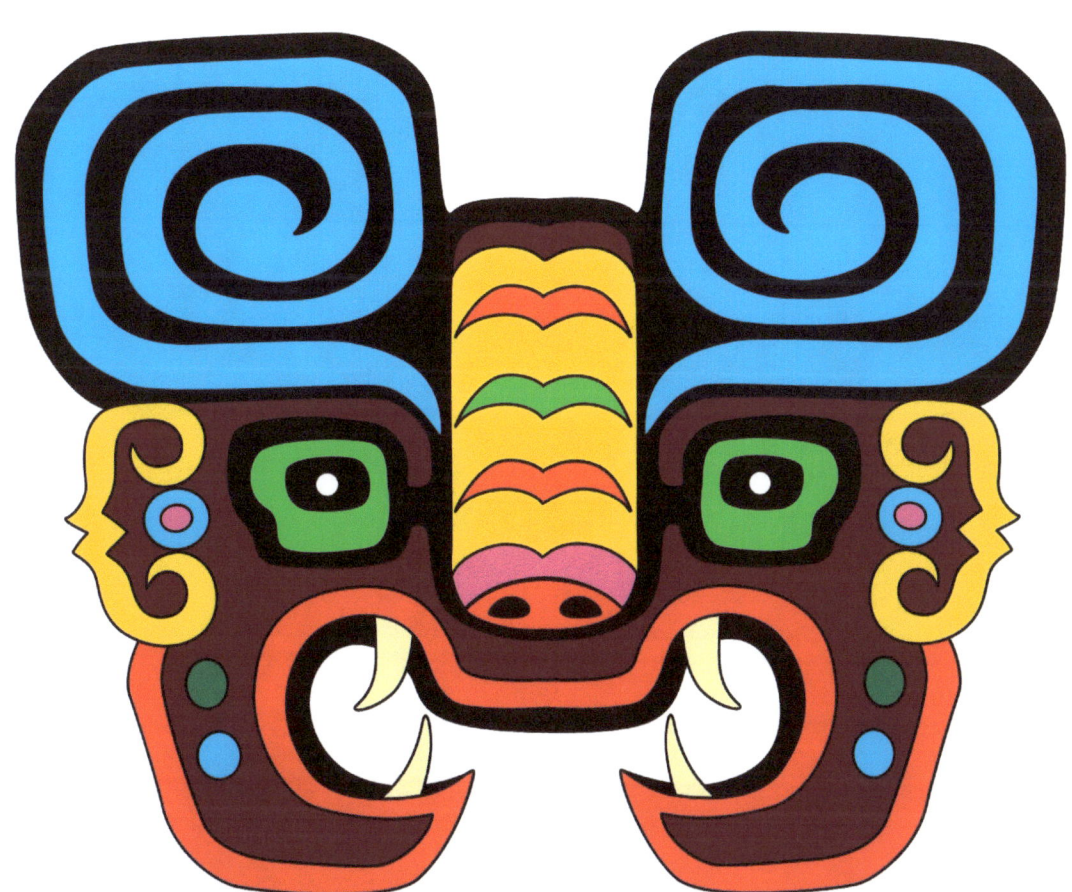

Bronze mask with fangs and horns, worn by the
Chinese warriors during 8th Century B.C.E. or earlier.

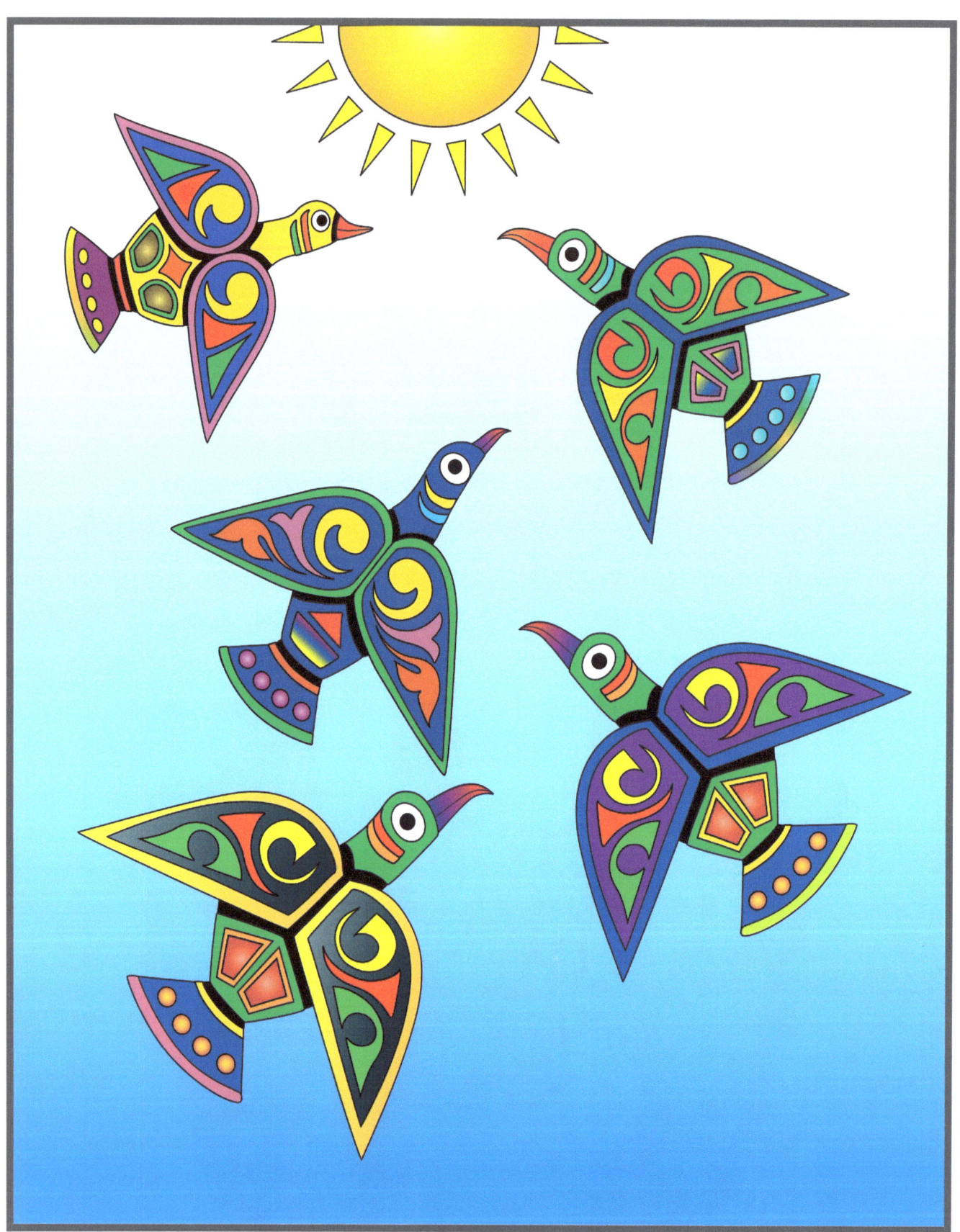

These highly stylized elegant birds are from a shield. Ming Dynasty, 1368 C.E. - 1644 C.E.

Chinese Art

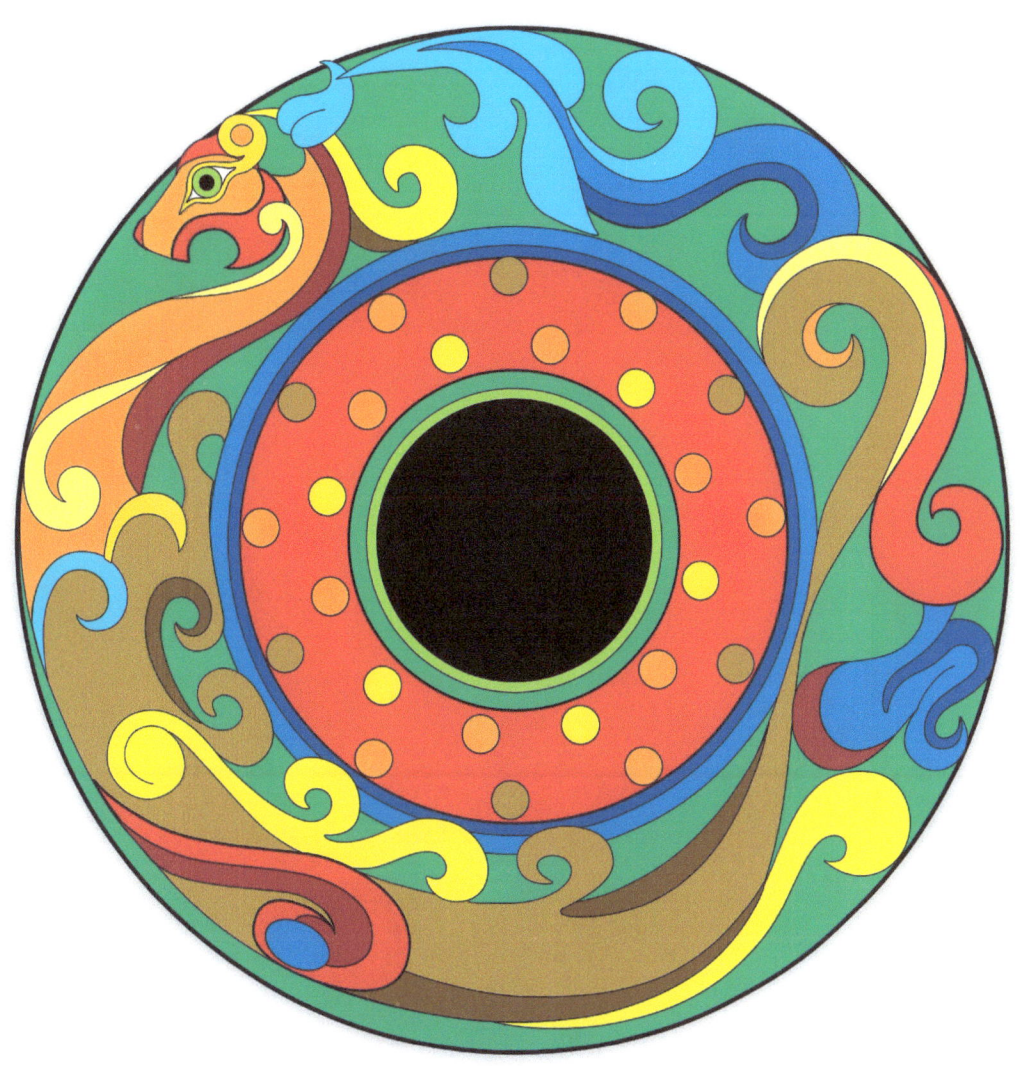

A concentric "Huan" Disc, decorated with dragons.
Warring States Period 475 B.C.E. - 221 B.C.E.

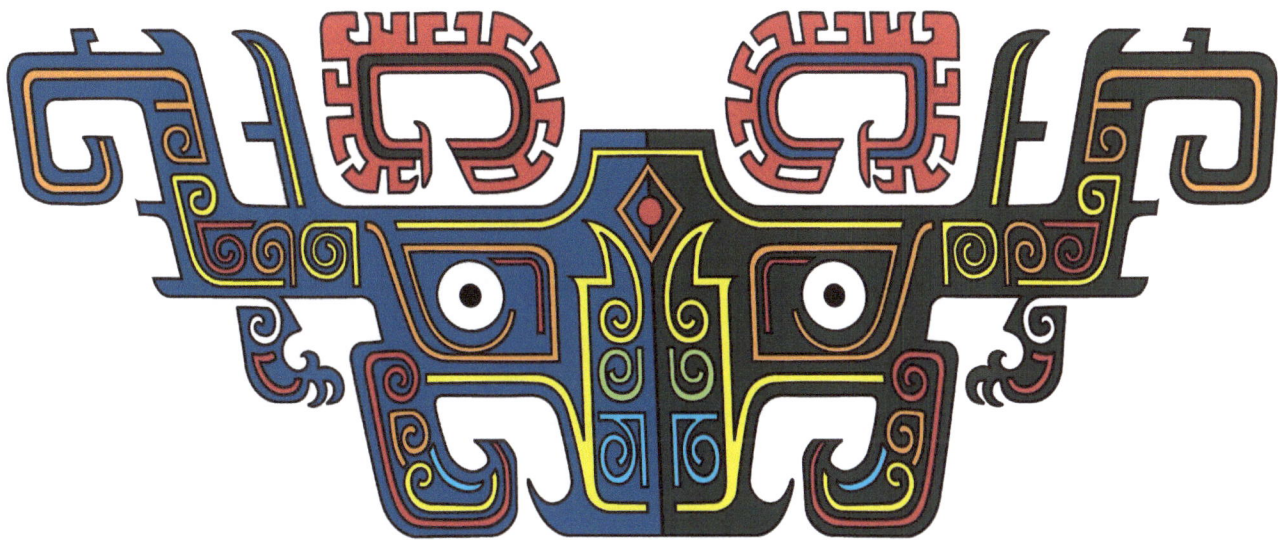

Decoration on Shang Bronzes named "taotic." Shang Dynasty- 1523 - 1028 B.C.E.

Funerary jar
Pottery with black slip.
Excavated at Banshan- Gansu.
Yangshao culture.

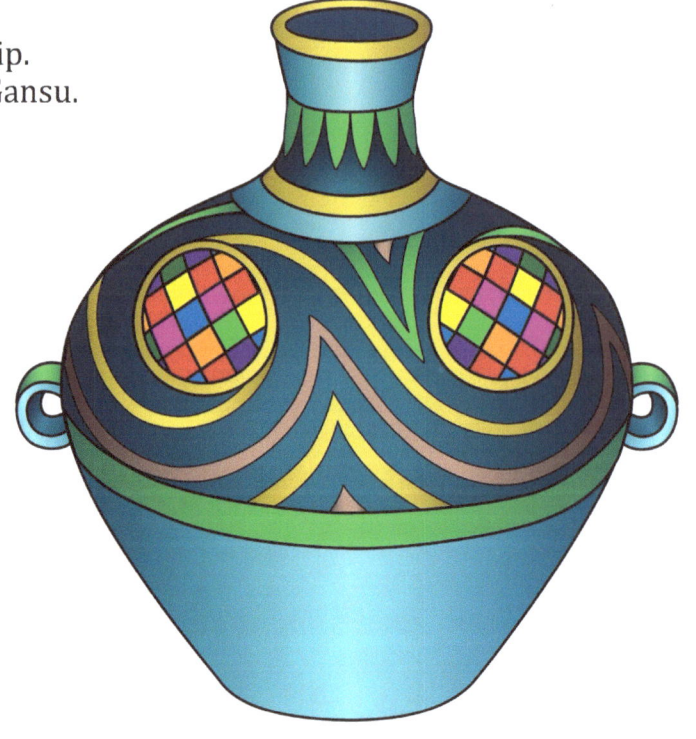

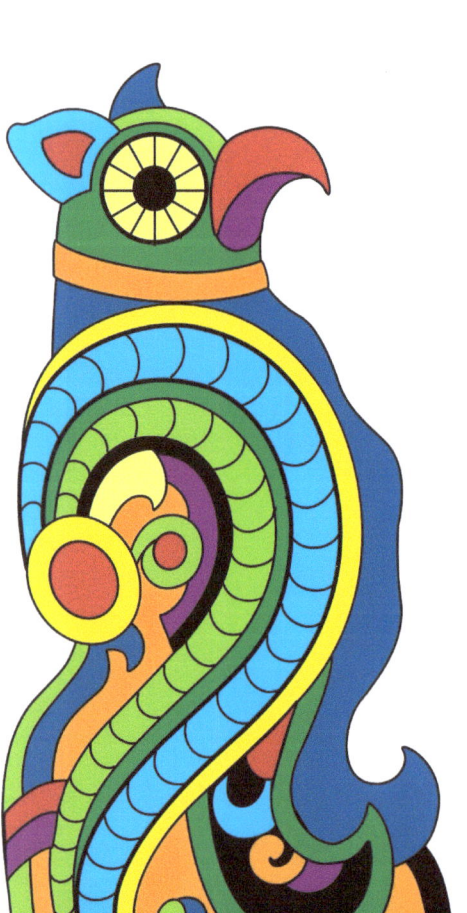

On Bronze Vessel, Niao - Tsun.
After Kwang Chih Chang.

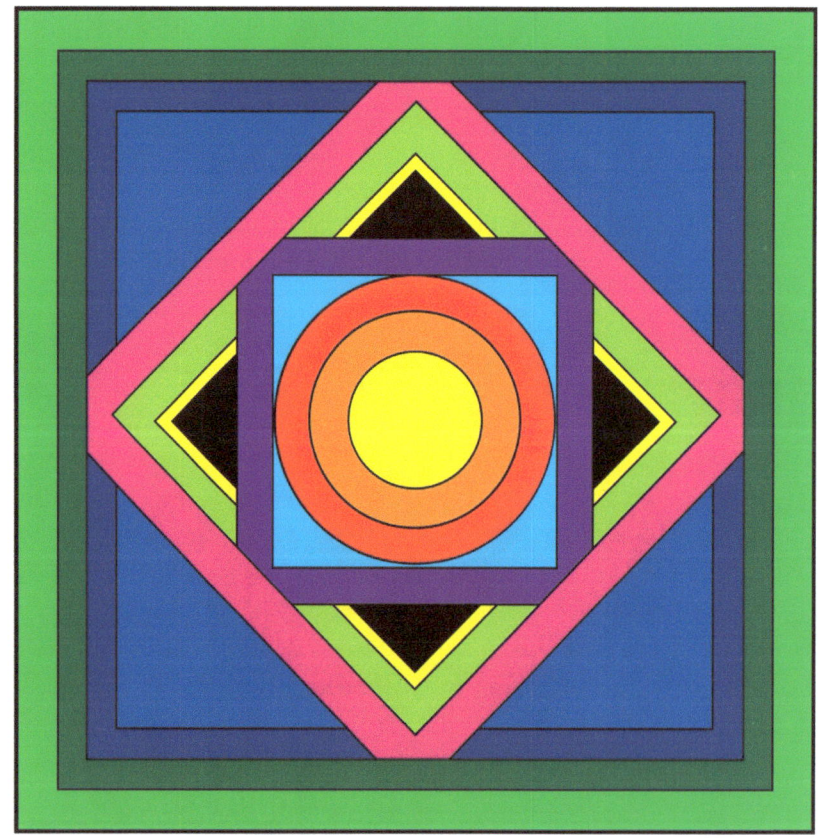

A painting with geometrical shapes on a lower part of a ceiling
in Cave Dunhuang. Wei Dynasty, 220 C.E. - 265 C.E.

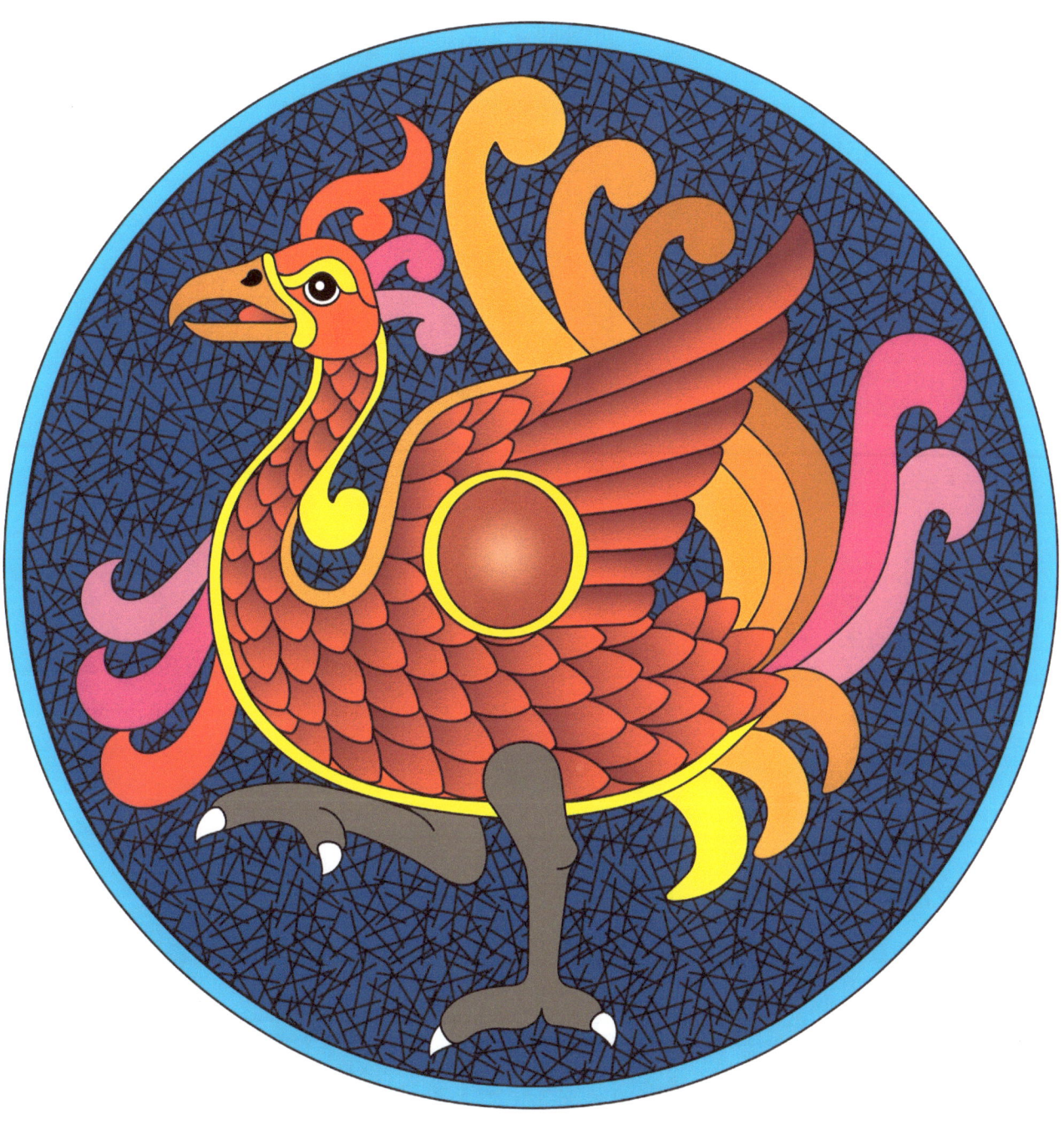

In a Liubo gaming board on stone, Zhongshan royal tomb
in Pingshan county. Warring States period, 475 B.C.E. - 221 B.C.E.

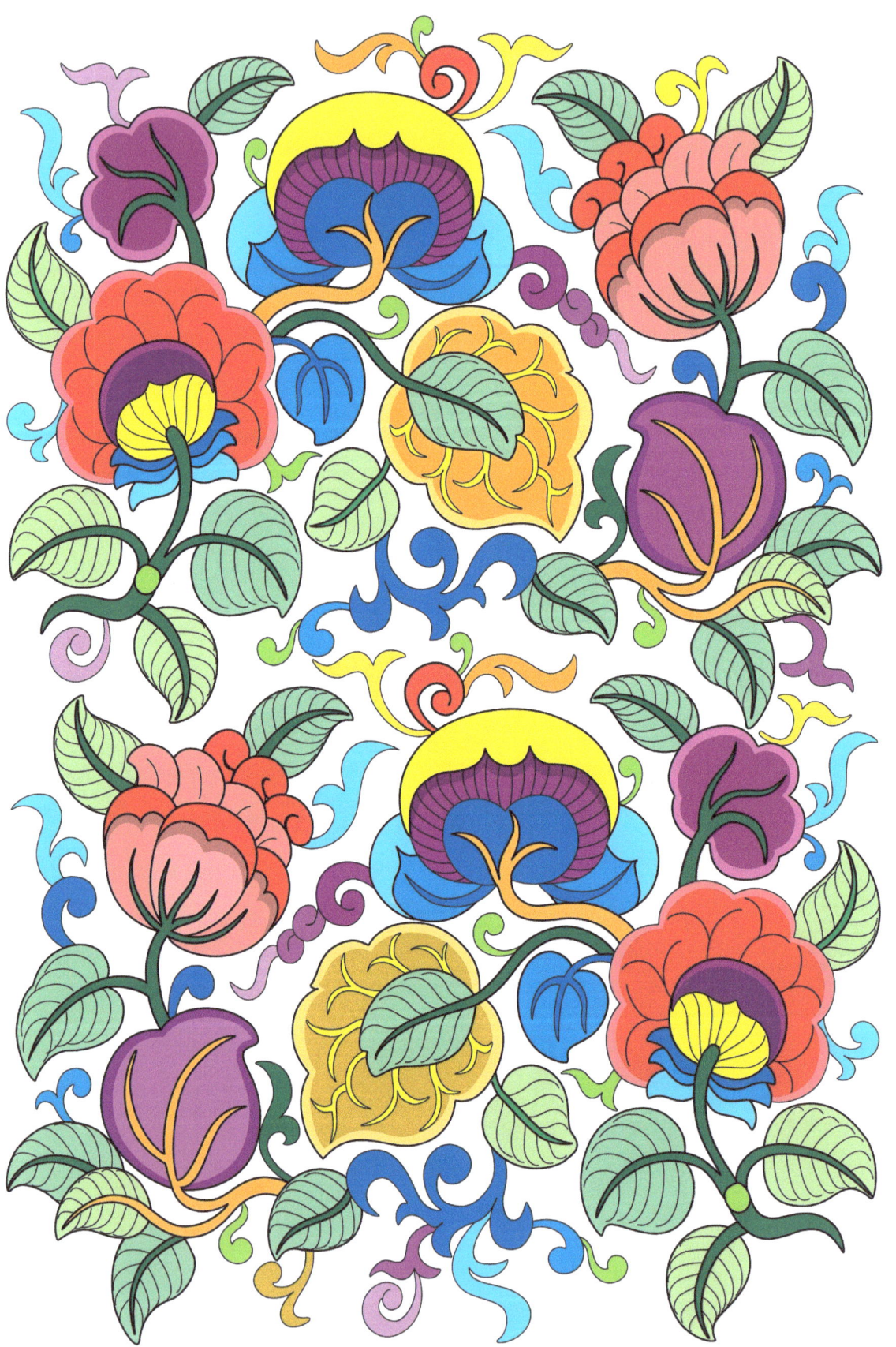

Floral drawing with peonies on a covered jar. The decoration
was traced in beaten silver, usually given as a gift. Tang Dynasty, 618 C.E. - 907 C.E.

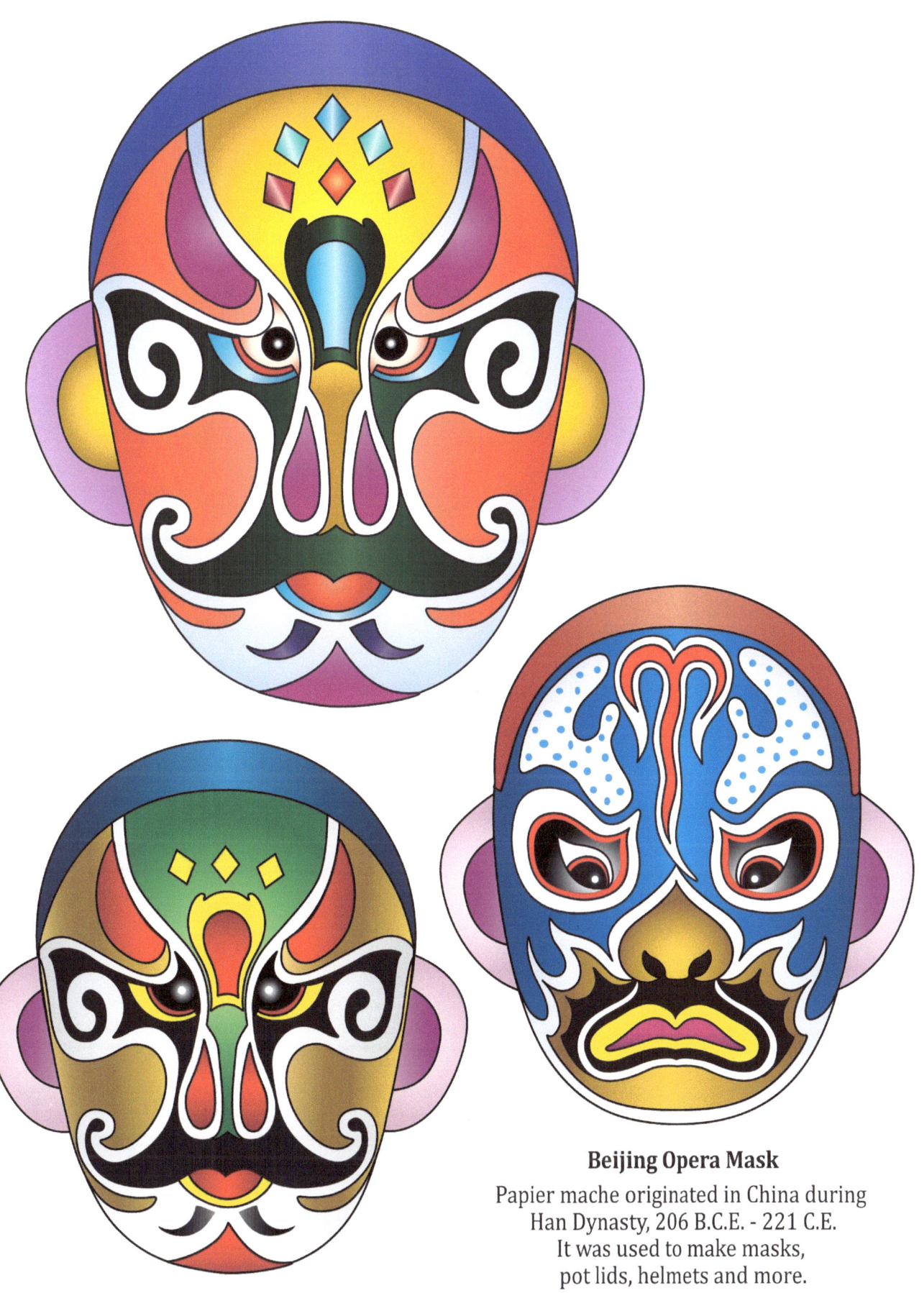

Beijing Opera Mask

Papier mache originated in China during
Han Dynasty, 206 B.C.E. - 221 C.E.
It was used to make masks,
pot lids, helmets and more.

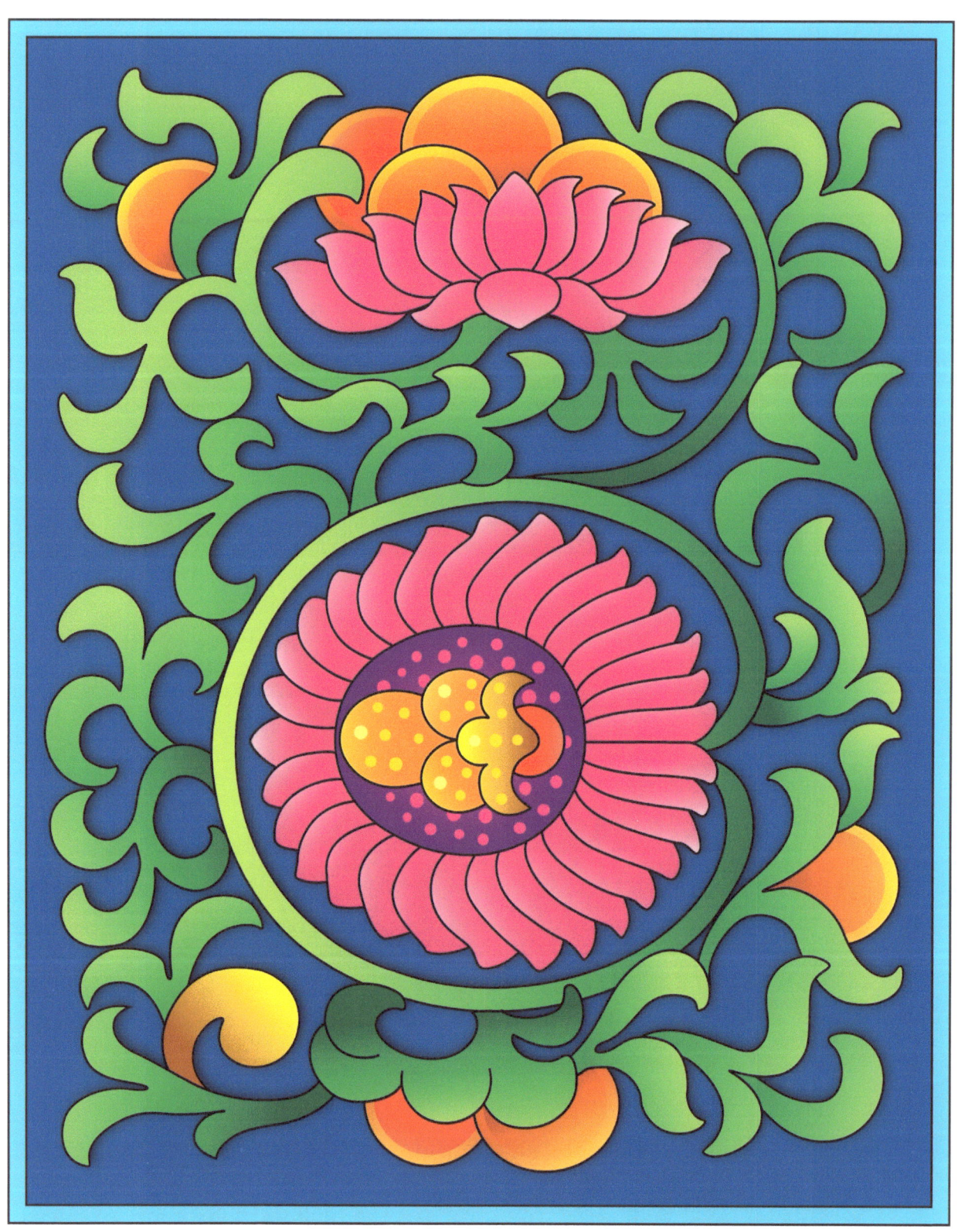

Floral decorating designs from a light
glaze to a darker slip on a pitcher. Northern Song Dynasty, 960 C.E. - 1127 C.E.

Chinese Dragon

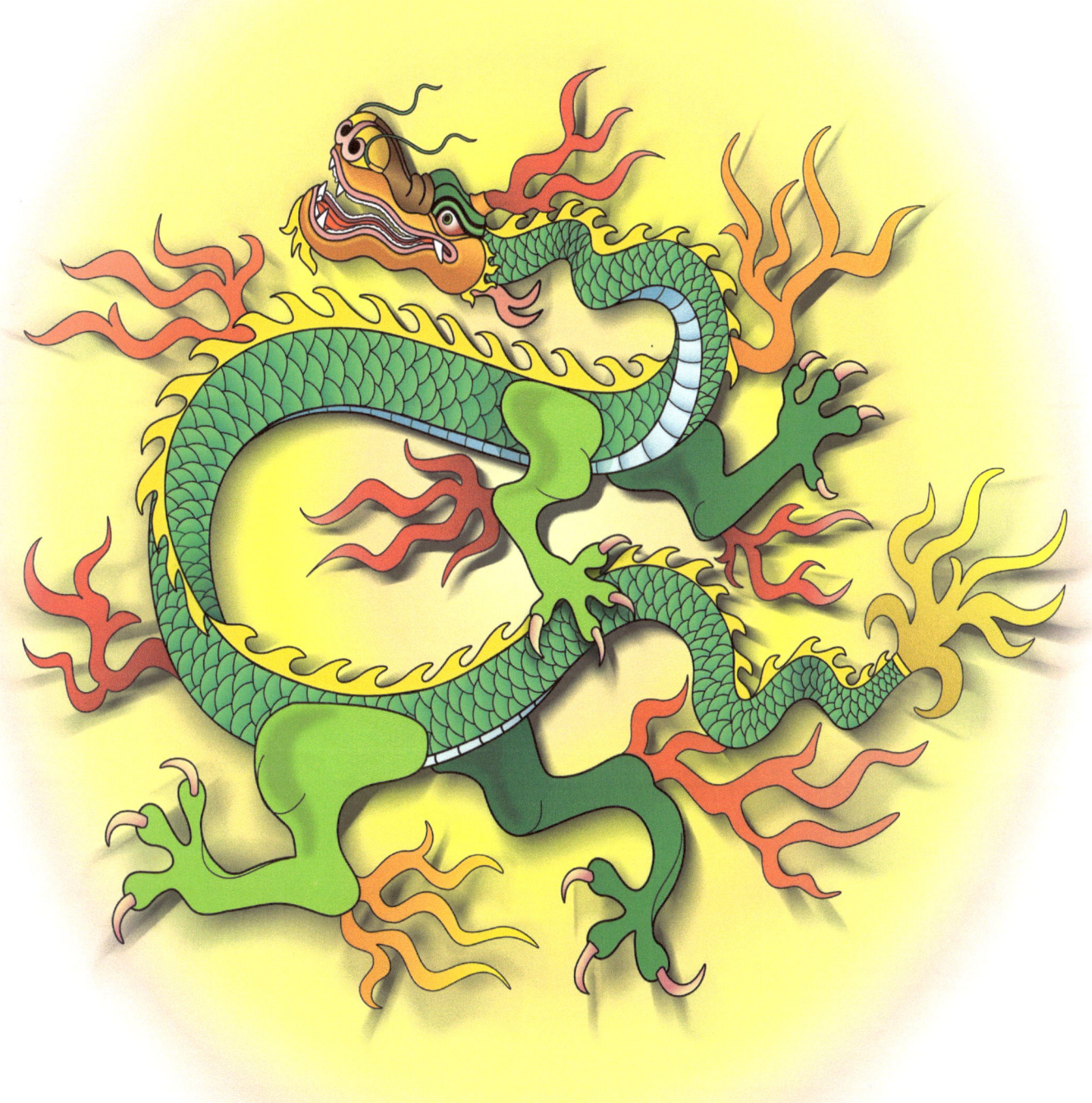

Dragon, from a Chinese porcelain. Ming Dynasty, 1368 C.E. - 1644 C.E.

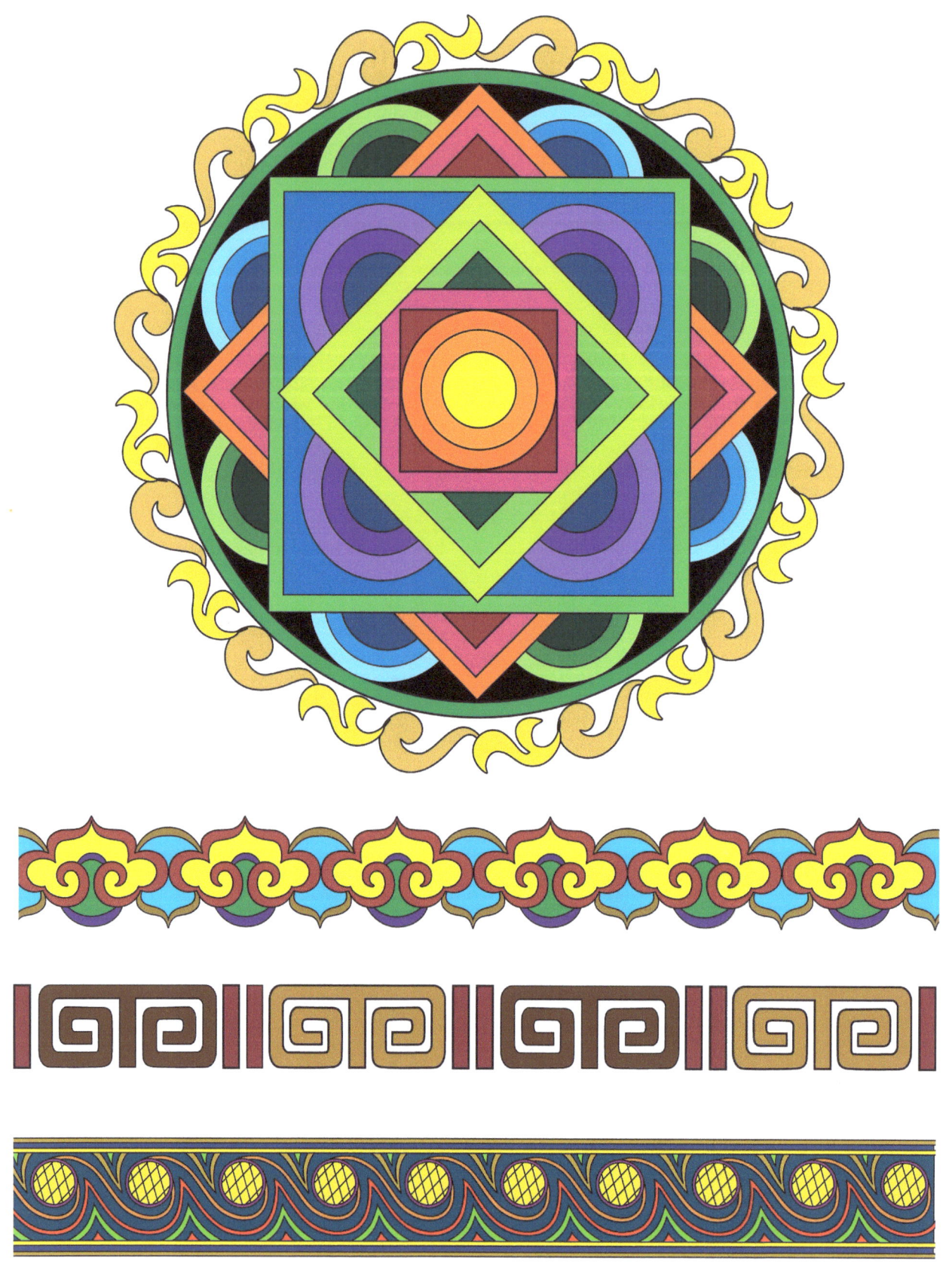

Examples of images created using the elements found in Chinese Art.

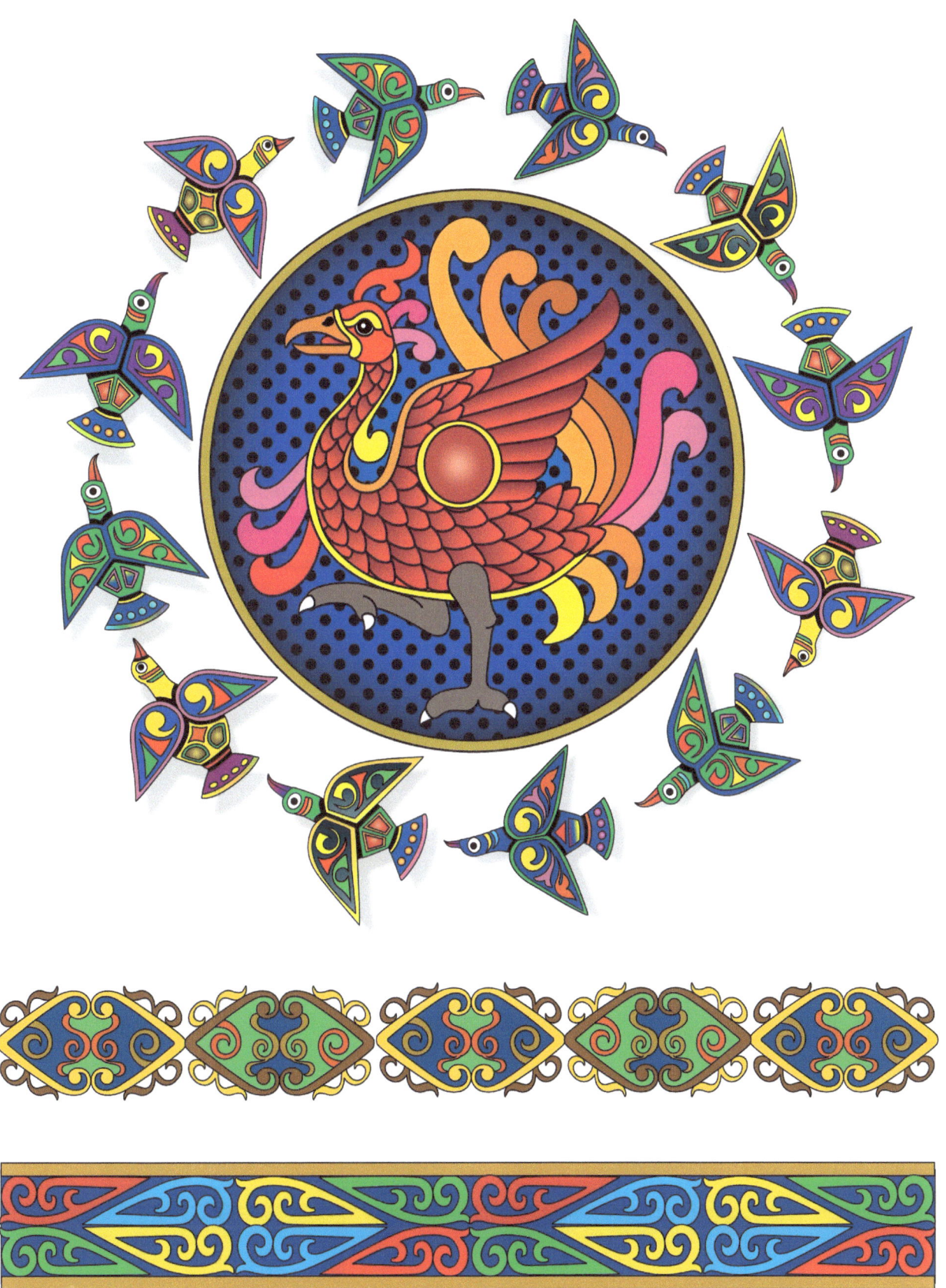

Examples of images created using the elements found in Chinese Art.

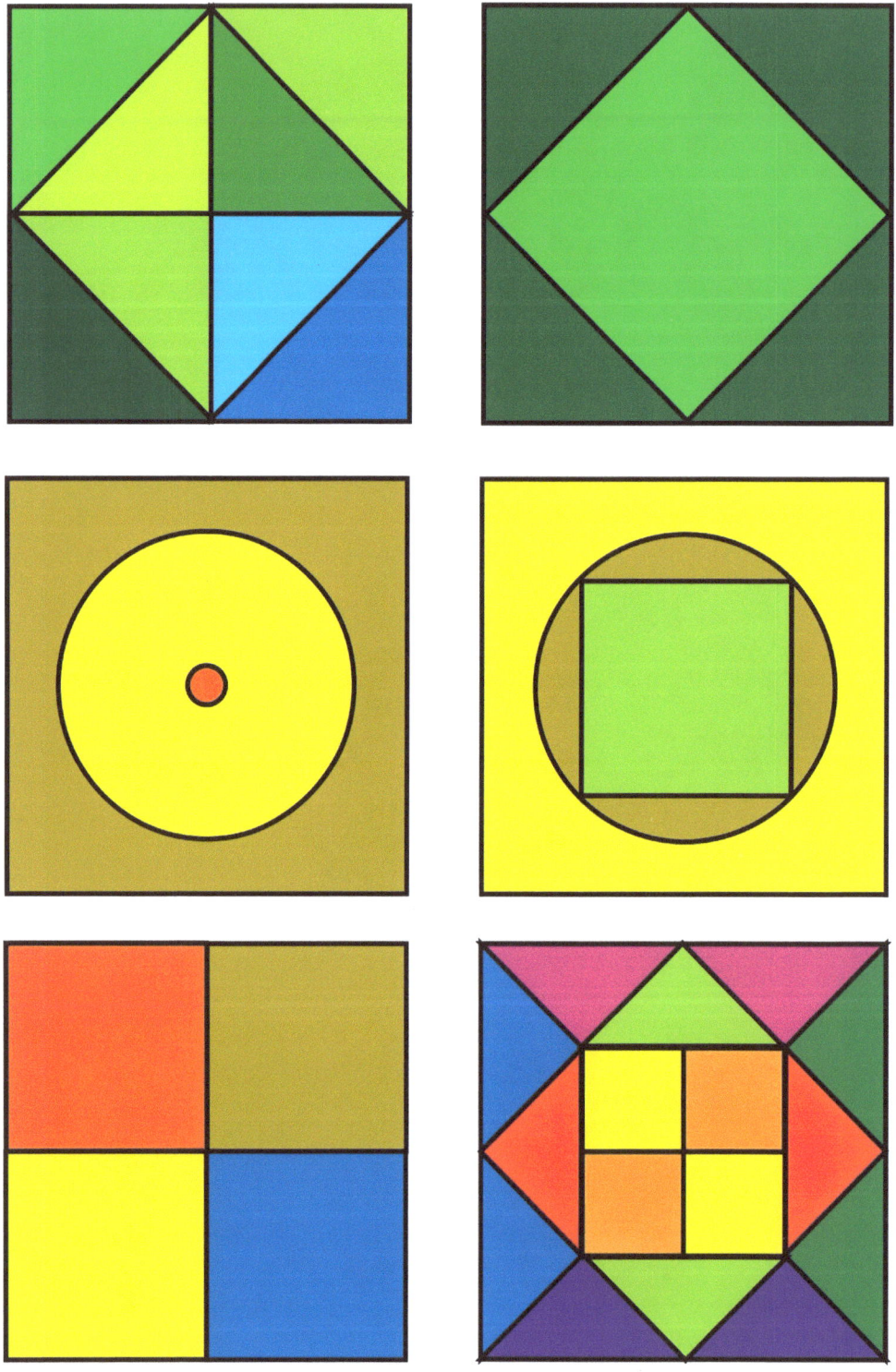

The ancient Babylonian Geometrical Tablets were used
to calculate the area of subdivisions of a square in the 1800 B.C.E.

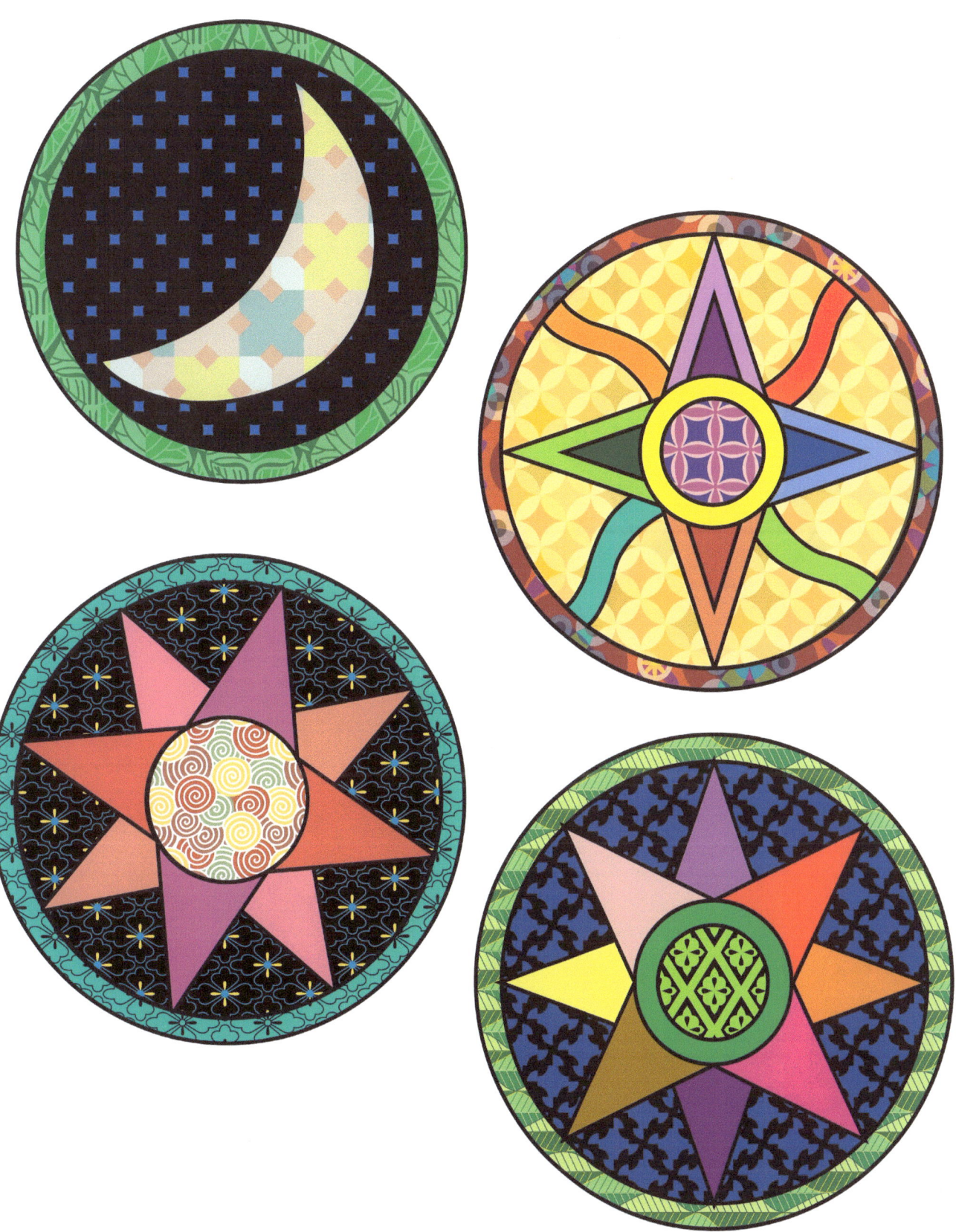

Symbols of God on stone, Kassites, Babylonia, 12th Century B.C.E.

Head of a ram from the time of
Mitannian domination at Alalakh.
15th - 14th Century B.C.E.

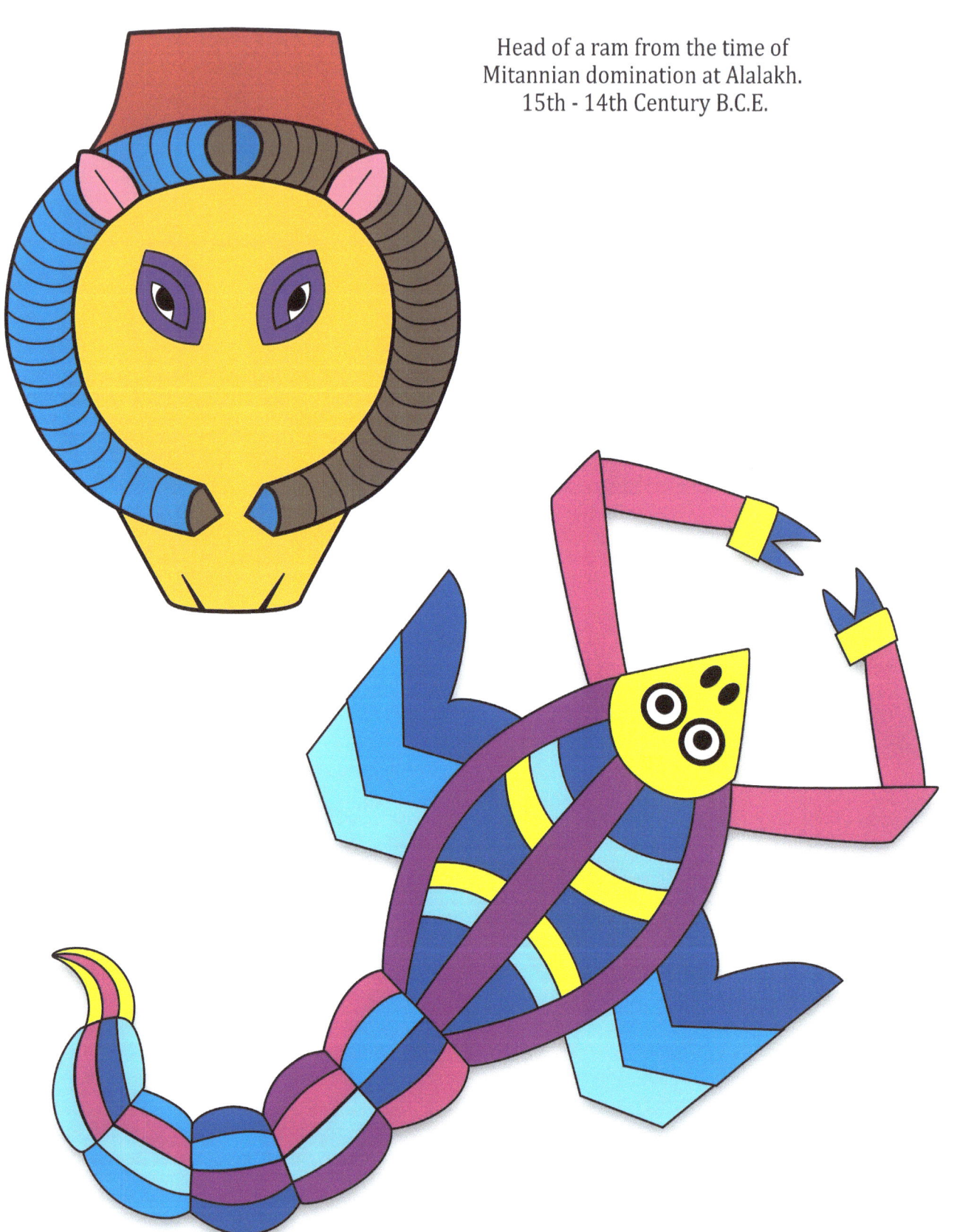

Scorpion as symbol of God invoked on a boundary stone, a type
introduced by the Kassites, during Babylonian Civilization, 1120 B.C.E.

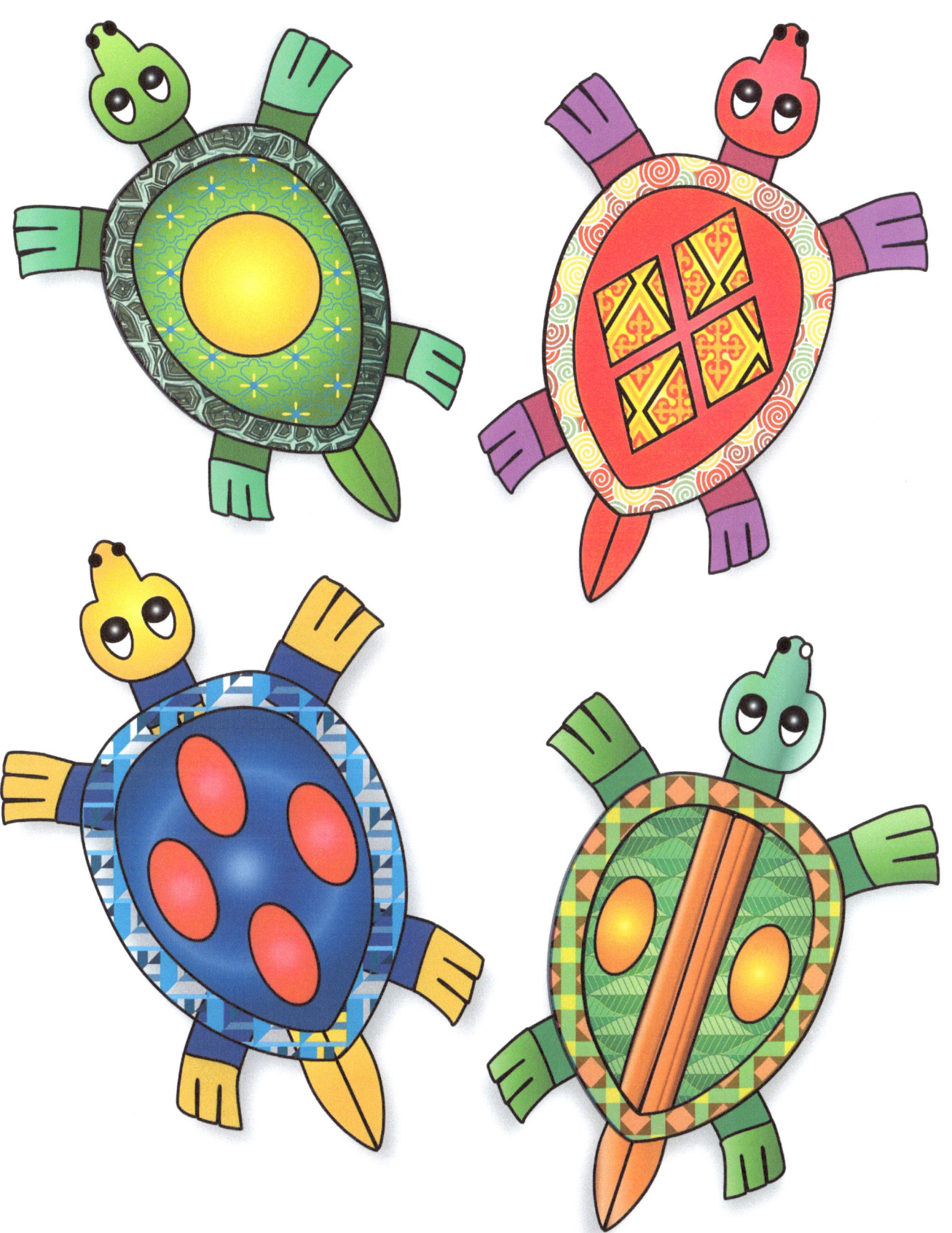

Turtles as ymbol of God on stone, Kassites, Babylonia- 1120 B.C.E.

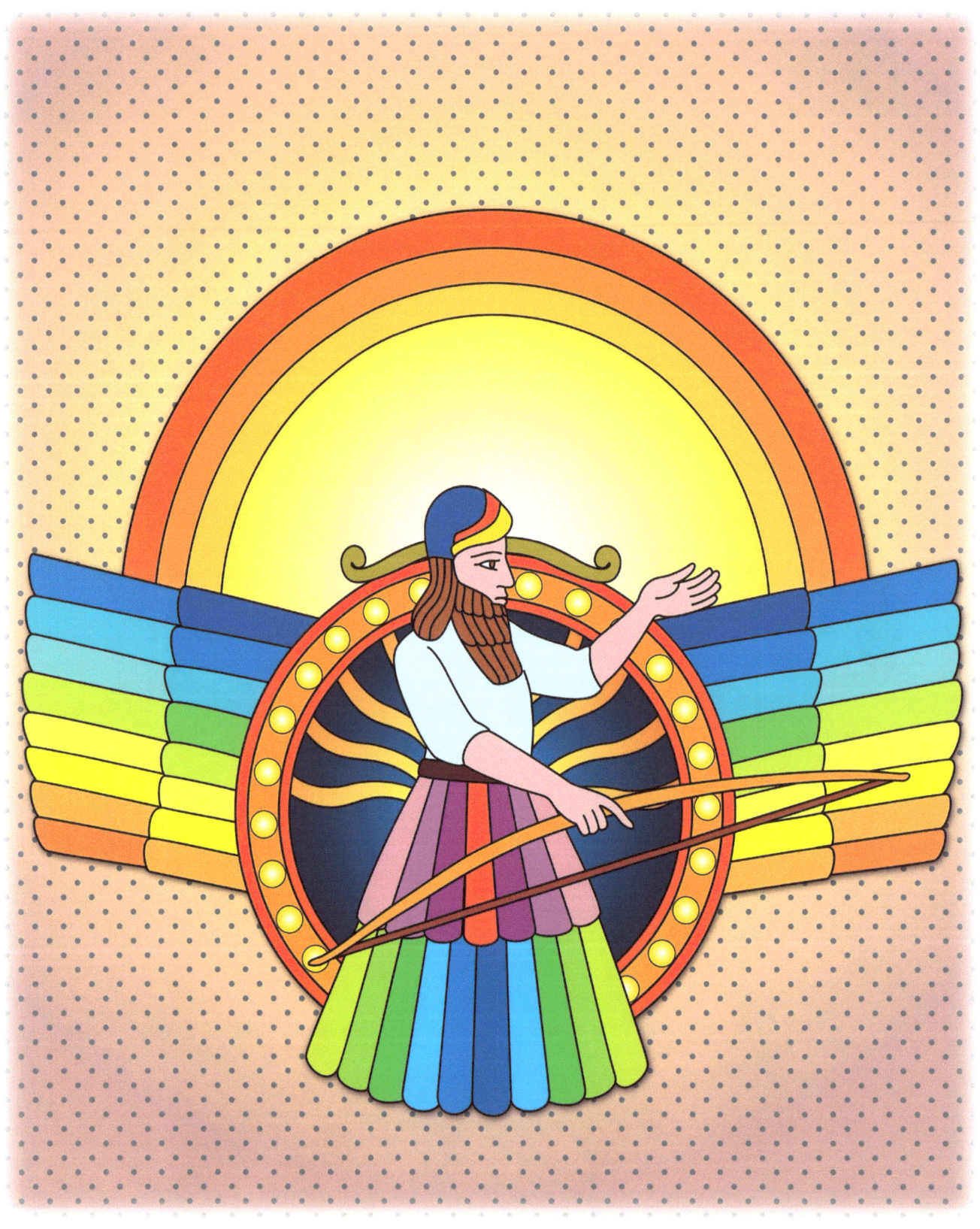

Assur, the Assyrian god on a sun-disk, 5th Century B.C.E.

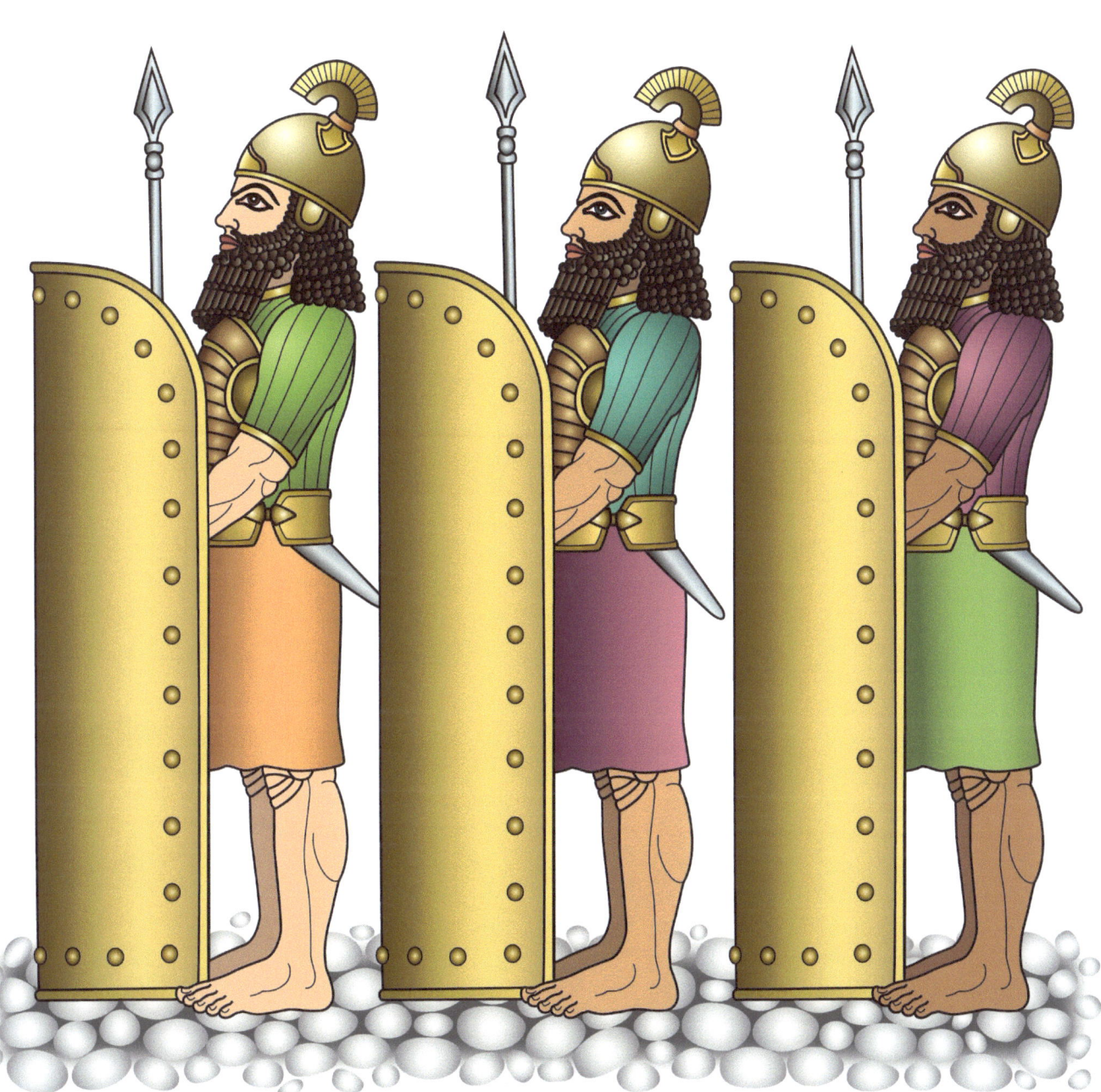

Assyrian King Ashurbanipal's soldiers (668 - 631 B.C.E.).

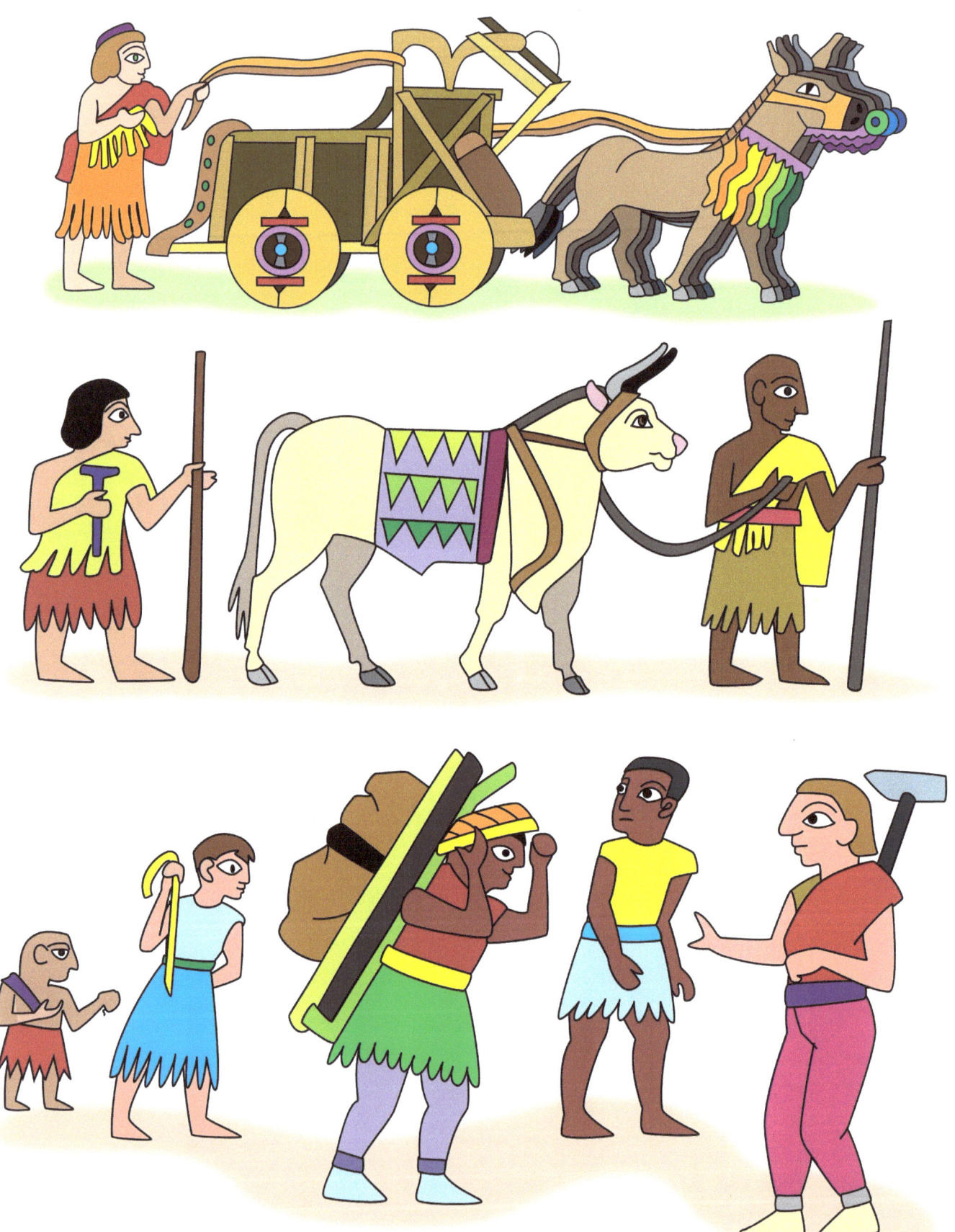

A victory celebration scene in Grave 779, when Ur (Urim) held the "kingship of Sumerian."

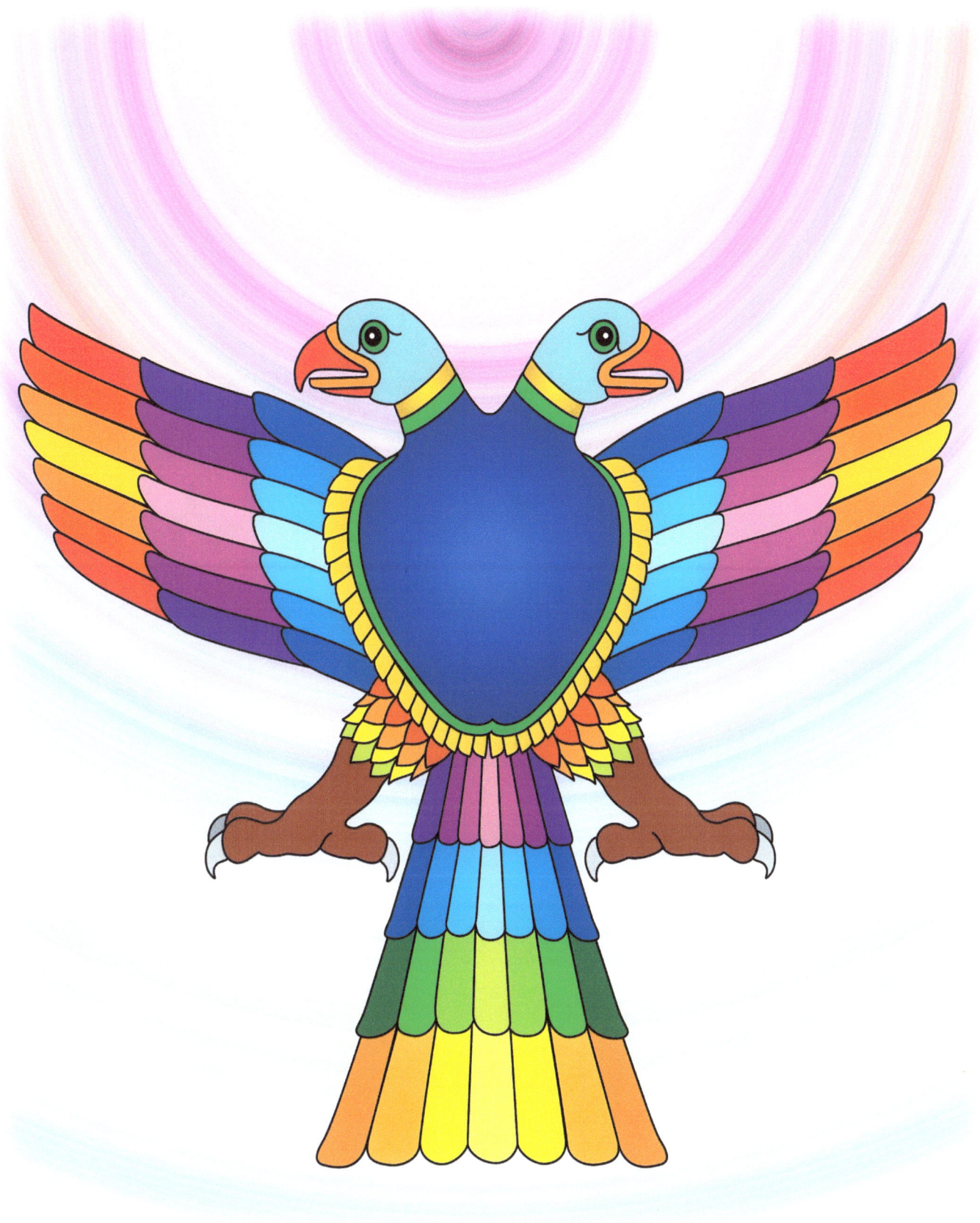

Double-headed eagle gripping two hares (not shown).
Relief from the Sphinx Gate at Alaca Huyuk. 14th Century B.C.E.

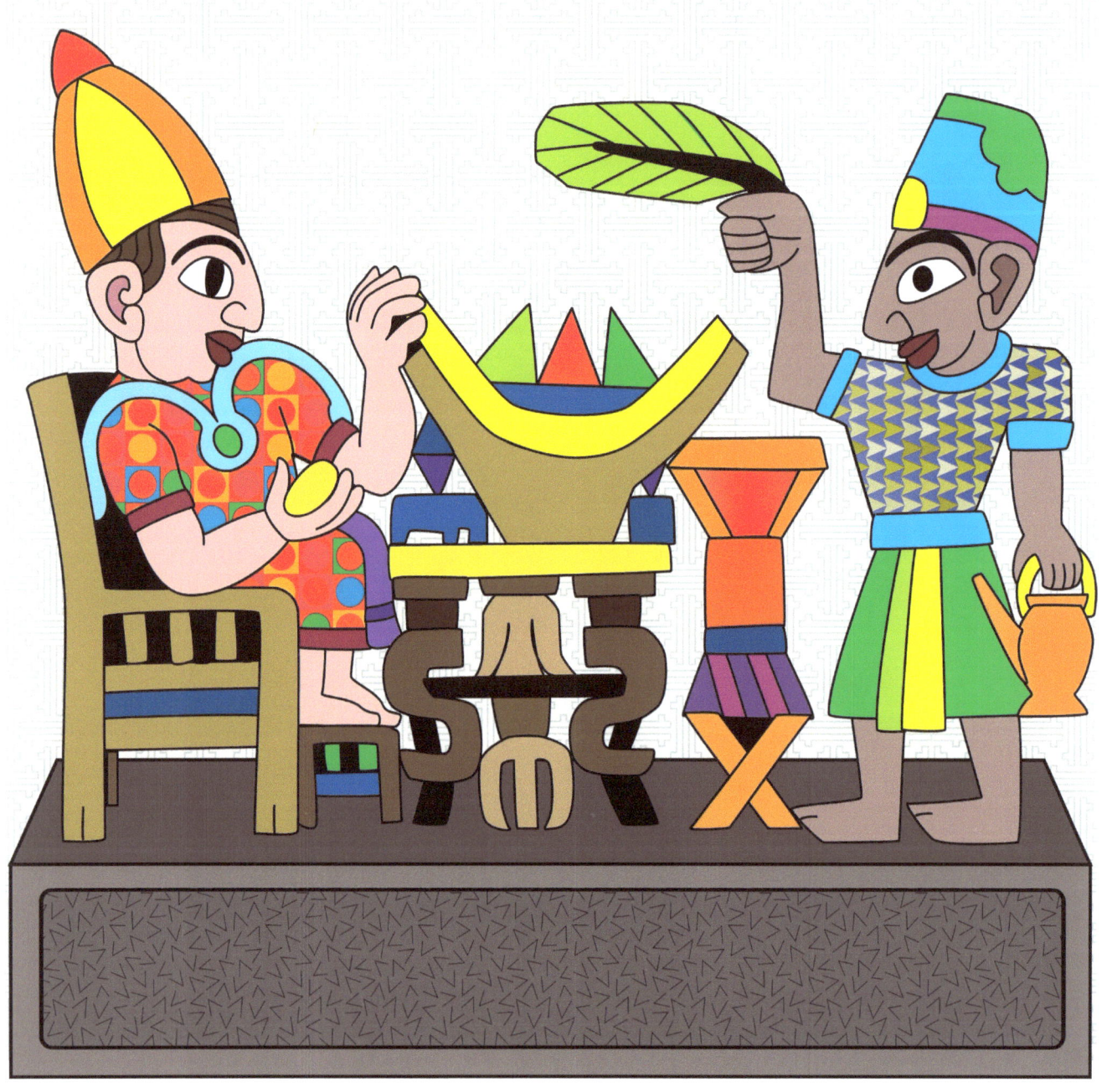

Part of a Neo-Hittite relief from the palace of Sanduarri in Karatepe, Cilicia.
The king is banqueting with the musicians.
A coarse imitation of Assyrian scenes. 7th Century B.C.E.

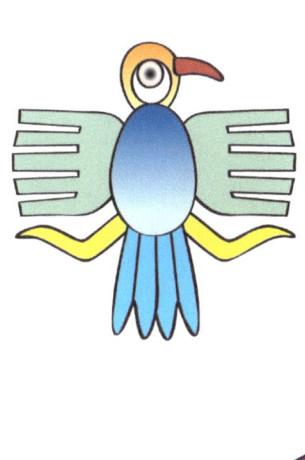
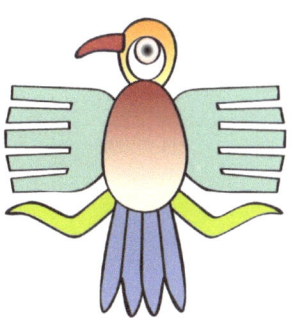

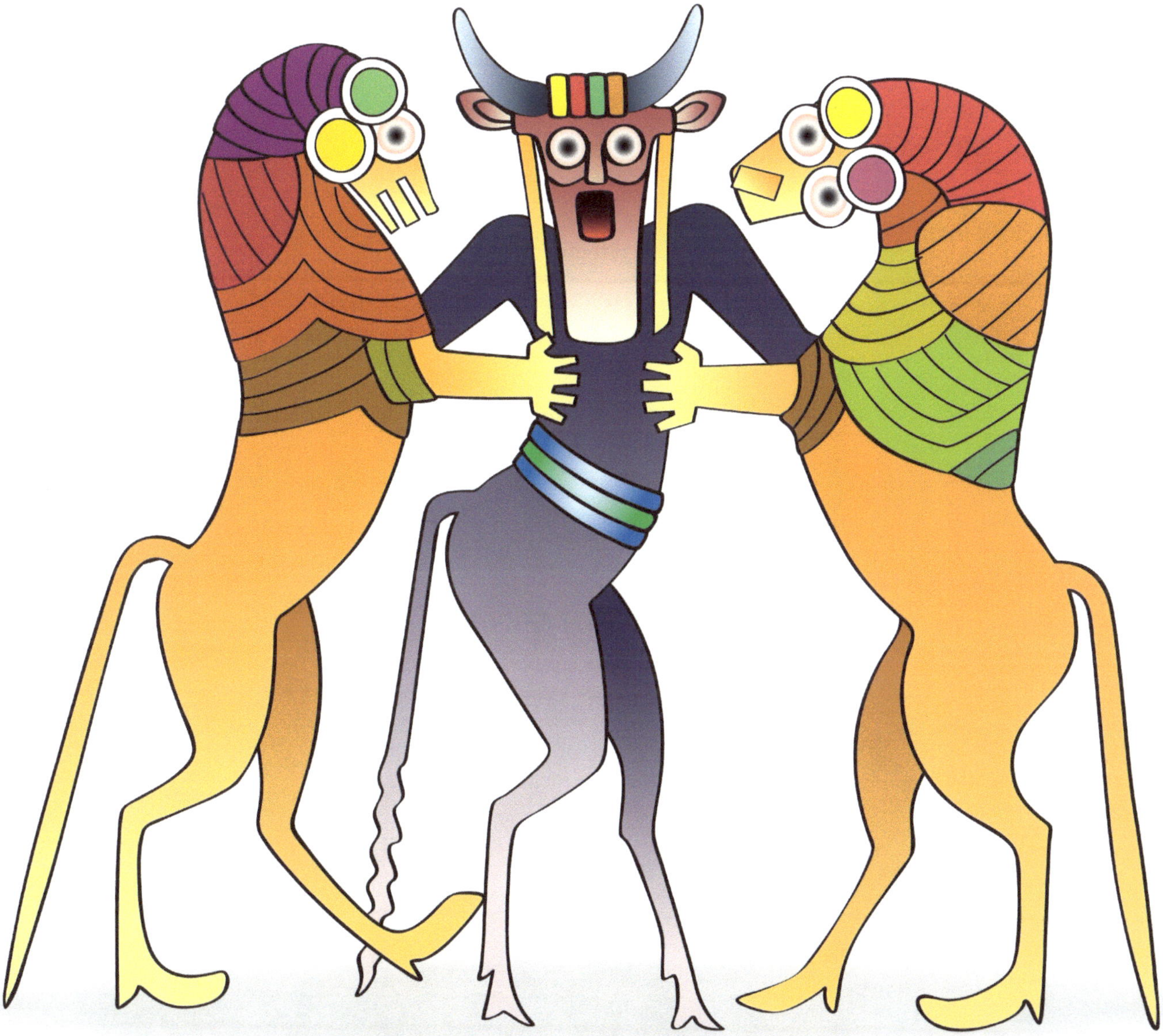

Early dynastic seal impression with animals
and mythological creatures. Between 2700 - 2370 B.C.E.

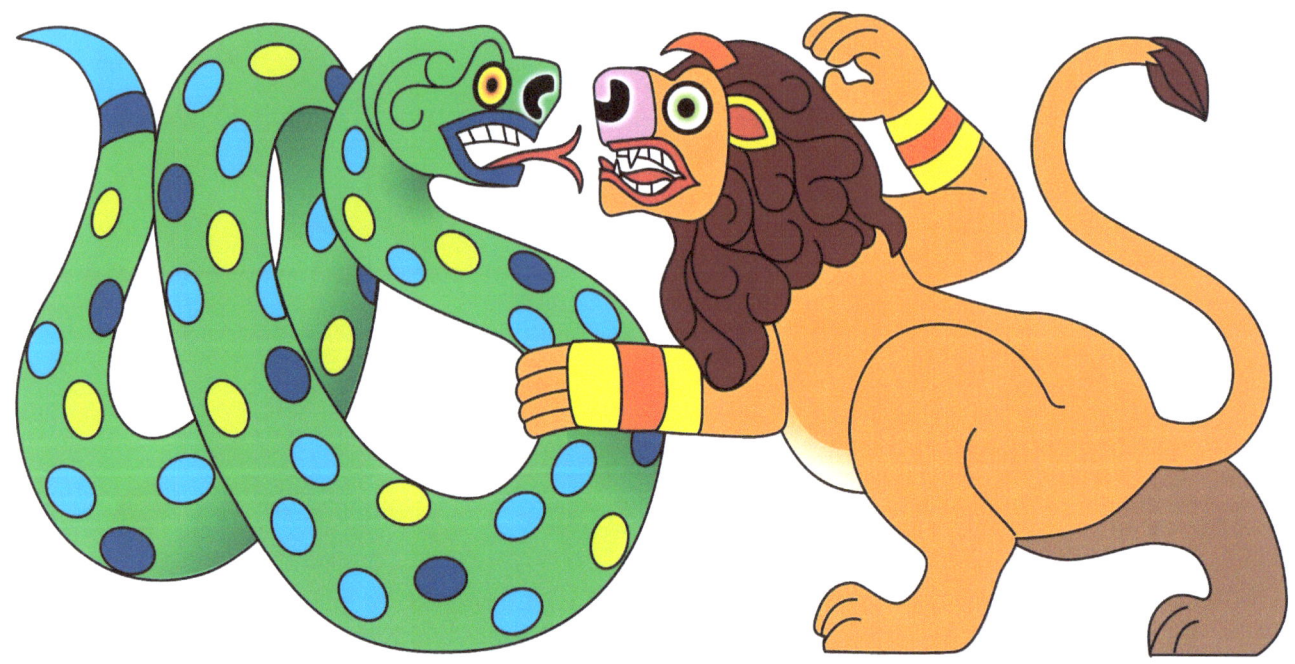

A combat between the king of snakes and the king of beasts.
On a stone bowl from Inanna Temple, Baghdad, 11th Century, B.C.E.

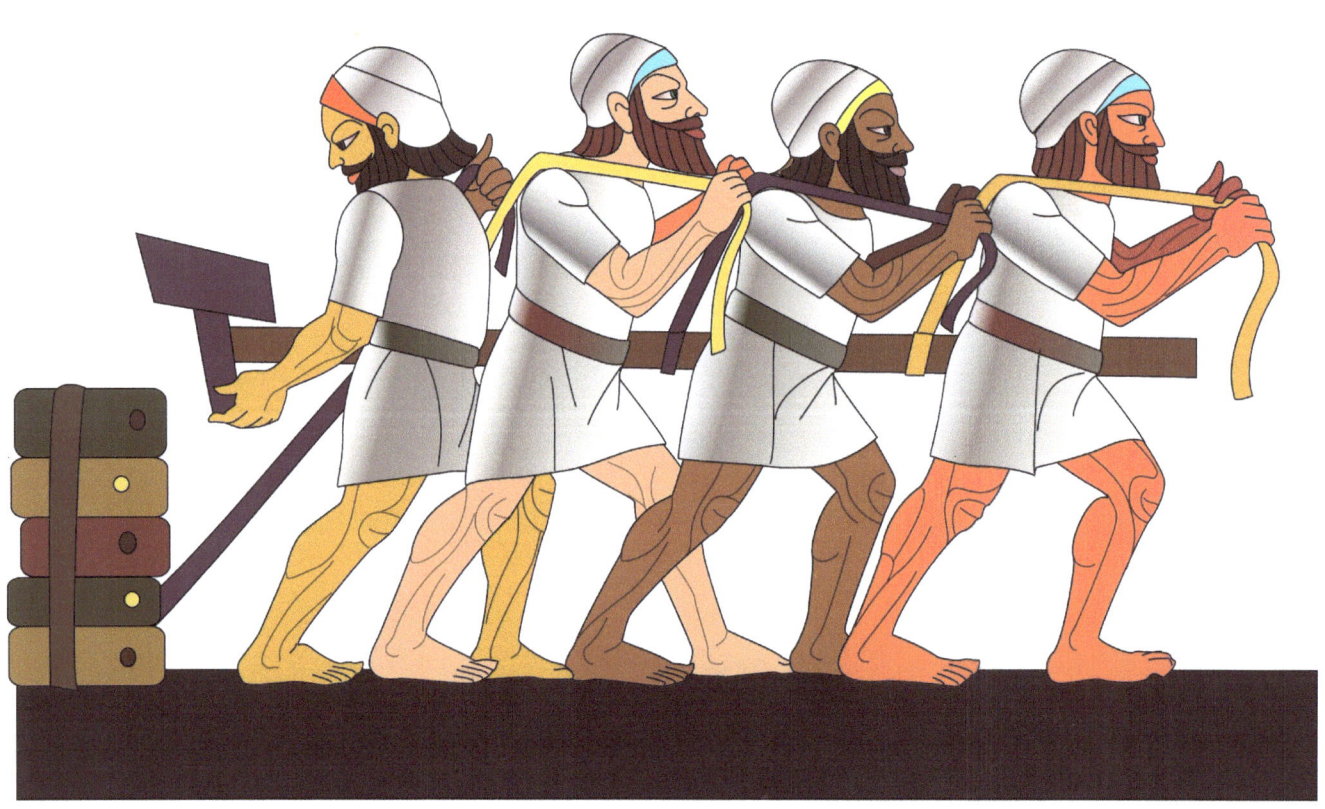

A relief work showing the deported populations hauling timber
to be used for roofing of Sargon's new capital at Khorsabad. Circa 6th Century B.C.E.

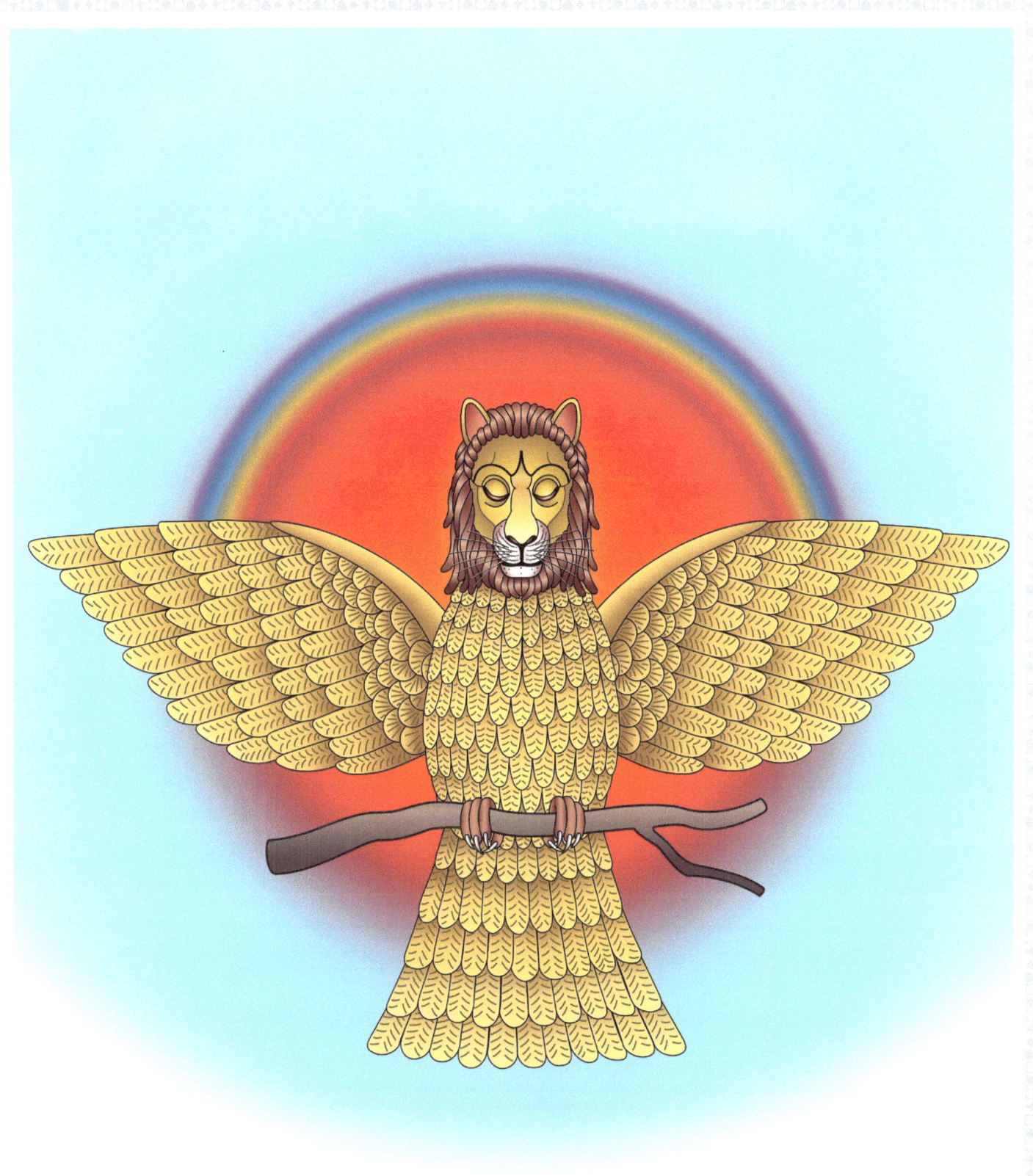

Imdugud, the Lion-headed eagle of Sumerian mythology with wings spread, 2600 - 2400 B.C.E.

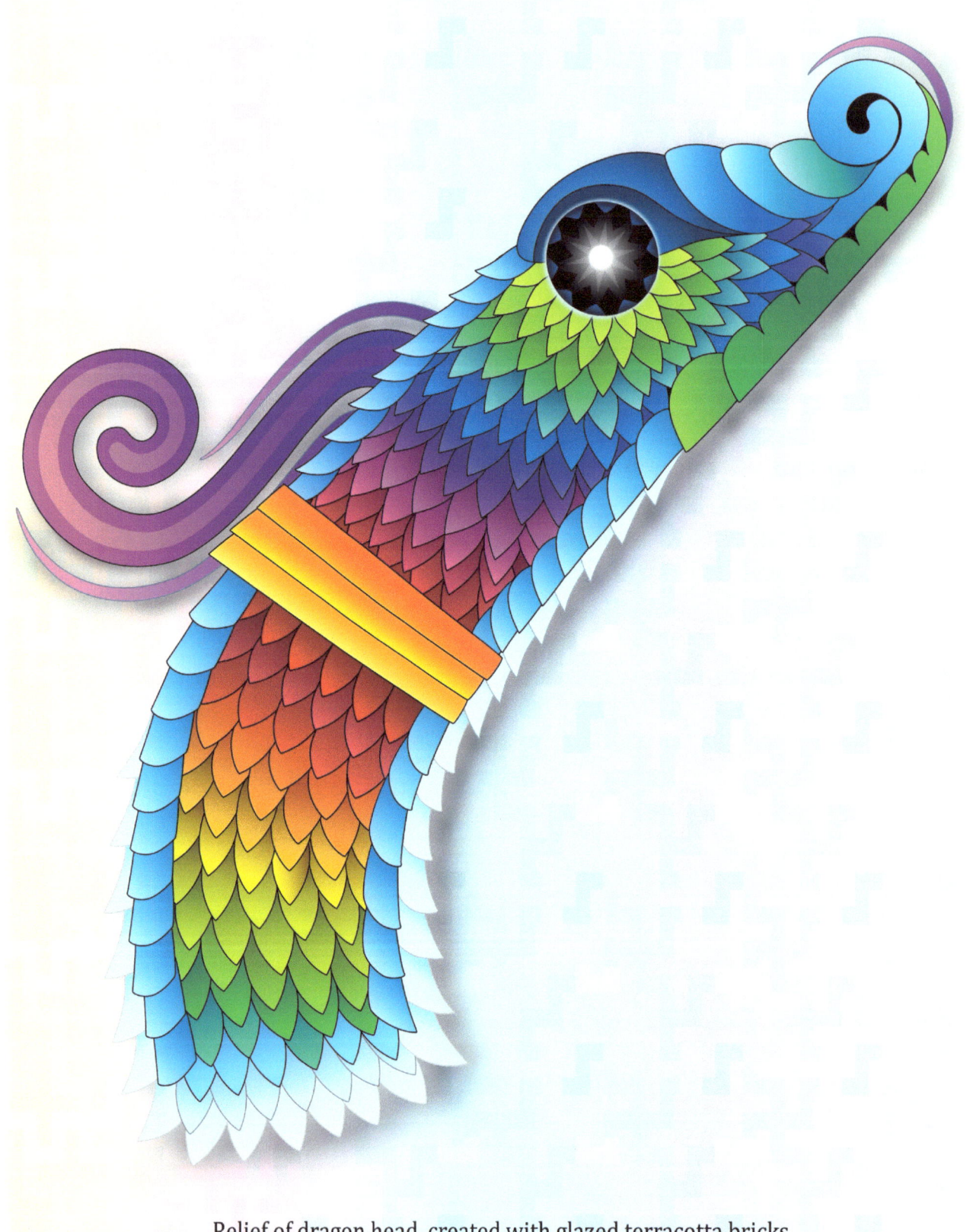

Relief of dragon head, created with glazed terracotta bricks
during King Nebuchadnezzar II reign, 605 - 562 B.C.E.

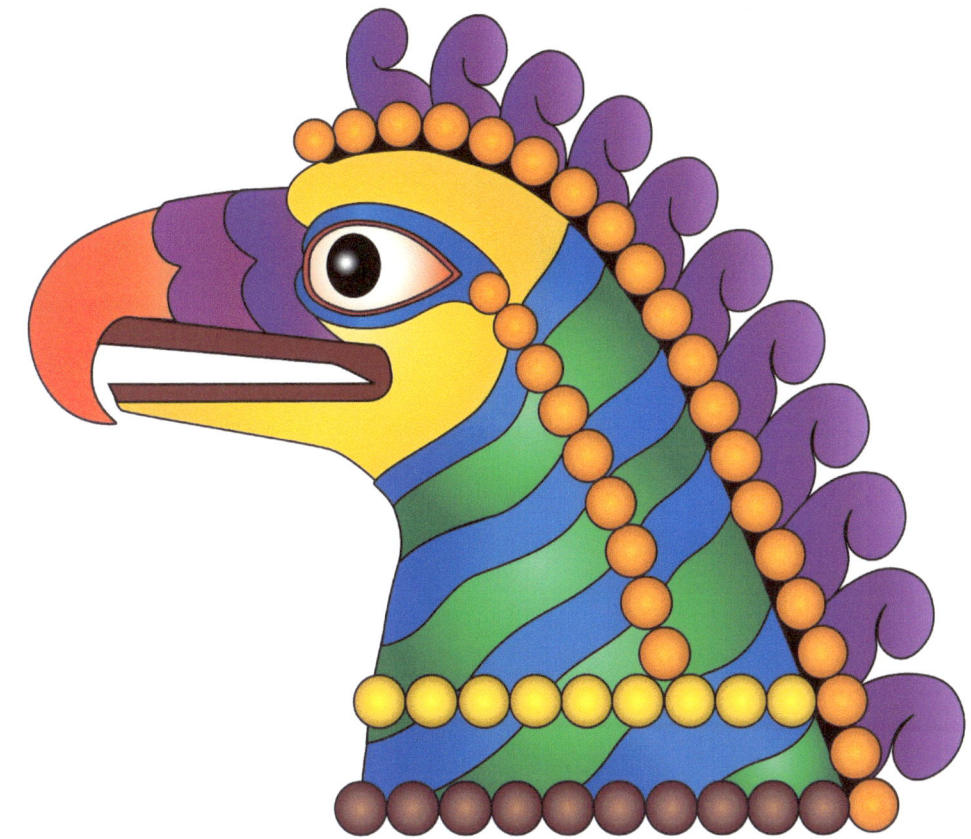

Eagle head of a genie. From a relief in inner room
lined with ritual scenes. Ashurnasirpal ceremonial room decoration.

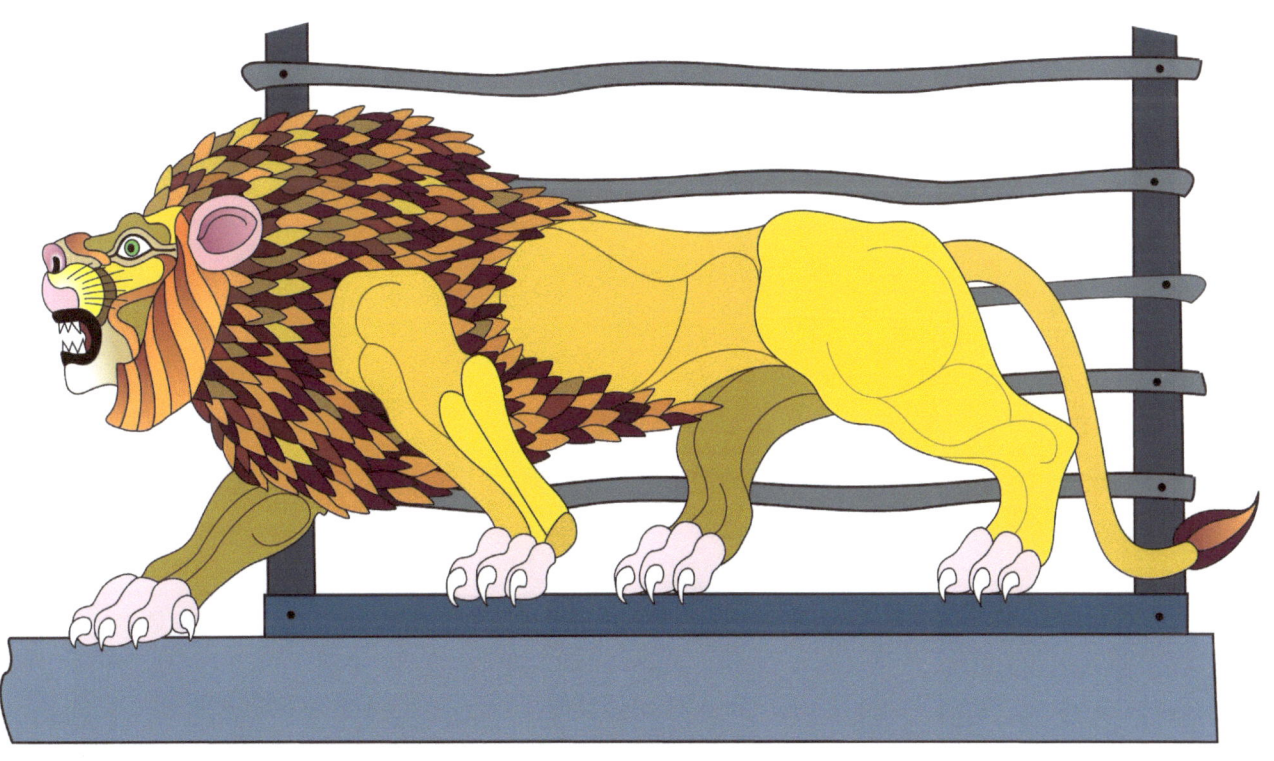

A Lion is released from its cage for King Ashurbanipal to hunt. 7th Century B.C.E.

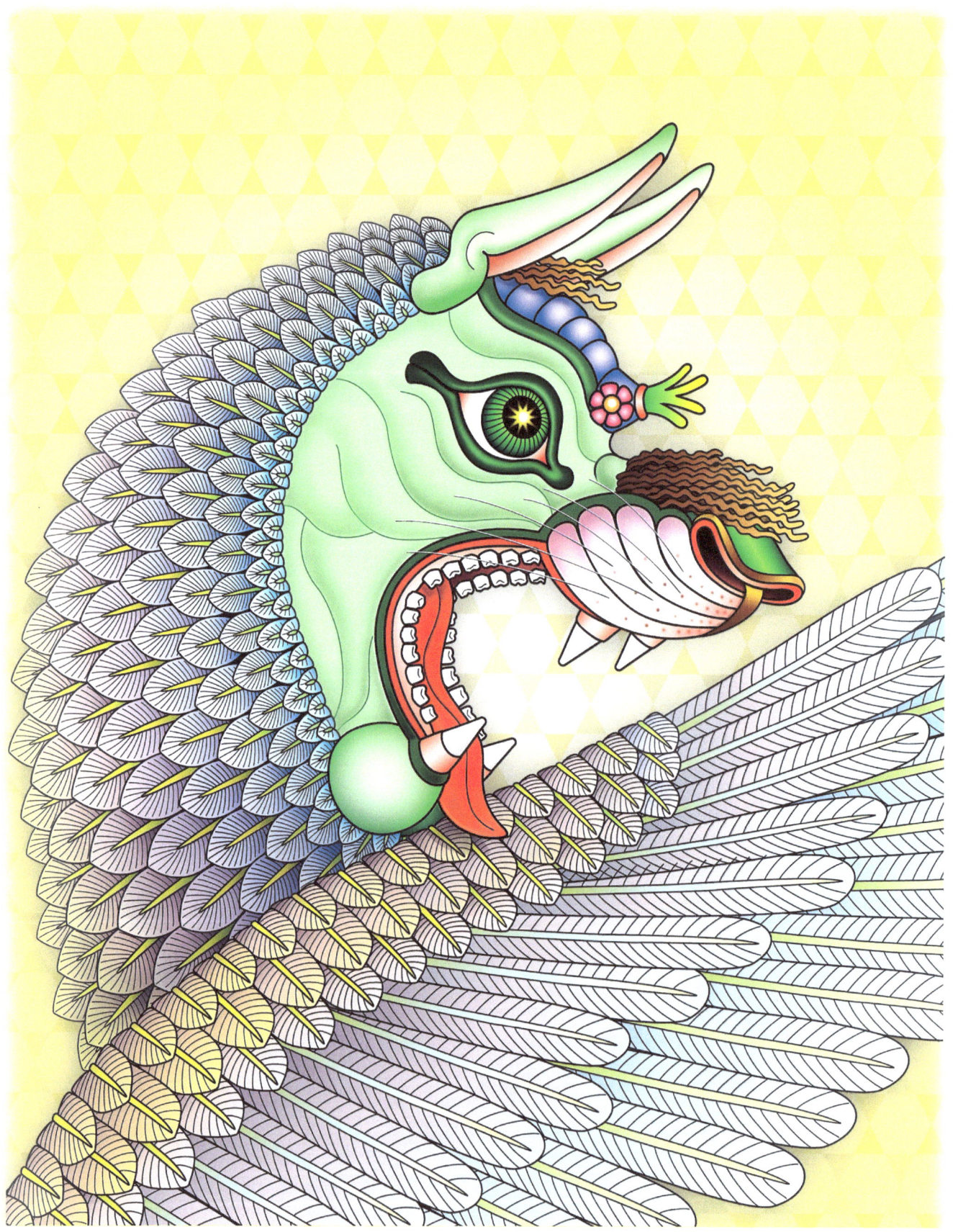

Winged Monster - a mythical character. Sculpted relief in one of Ashurbanipal room.

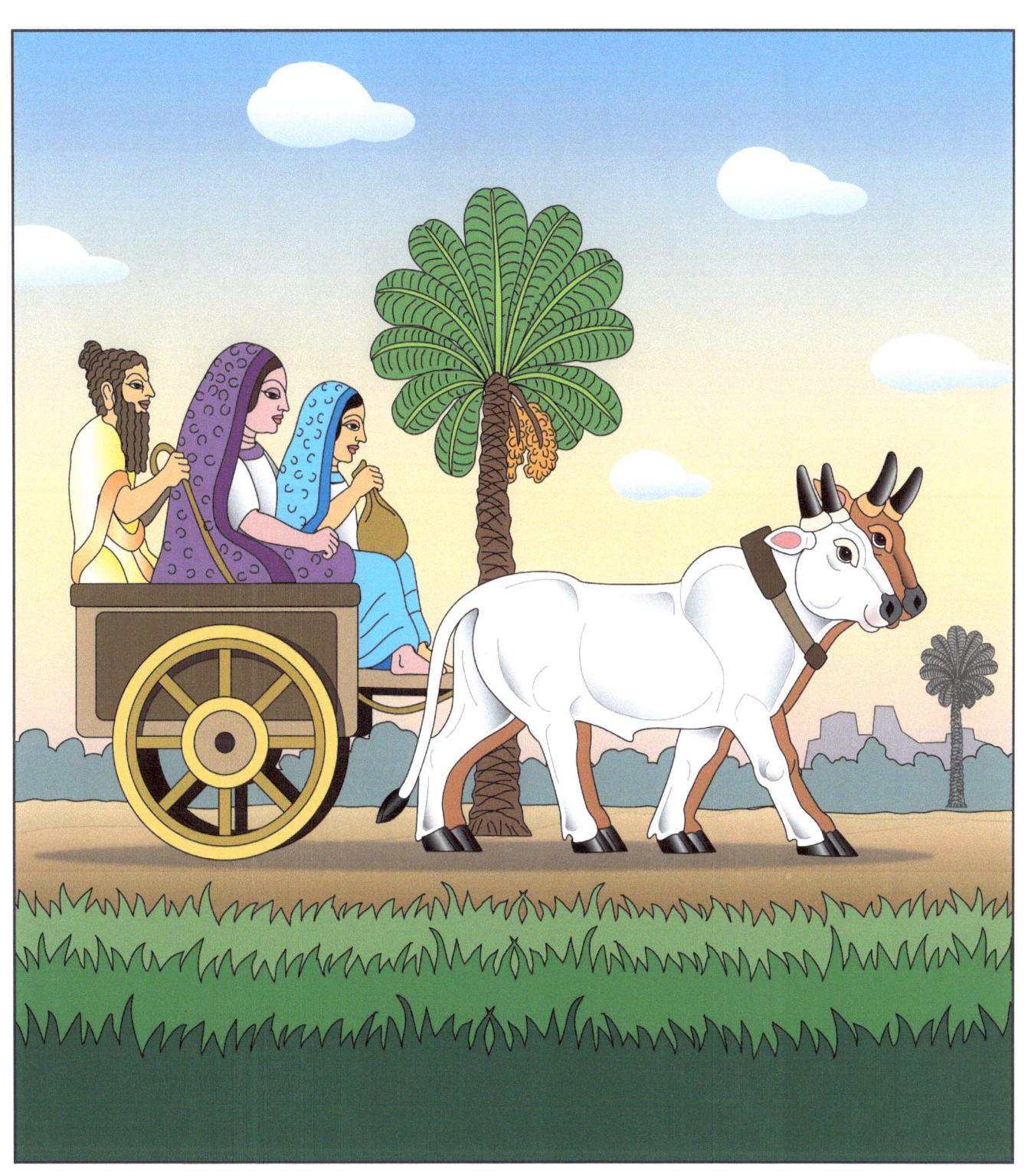

A relief on Tiglath-Pileser III. Nimrud, 730 B.C.E.

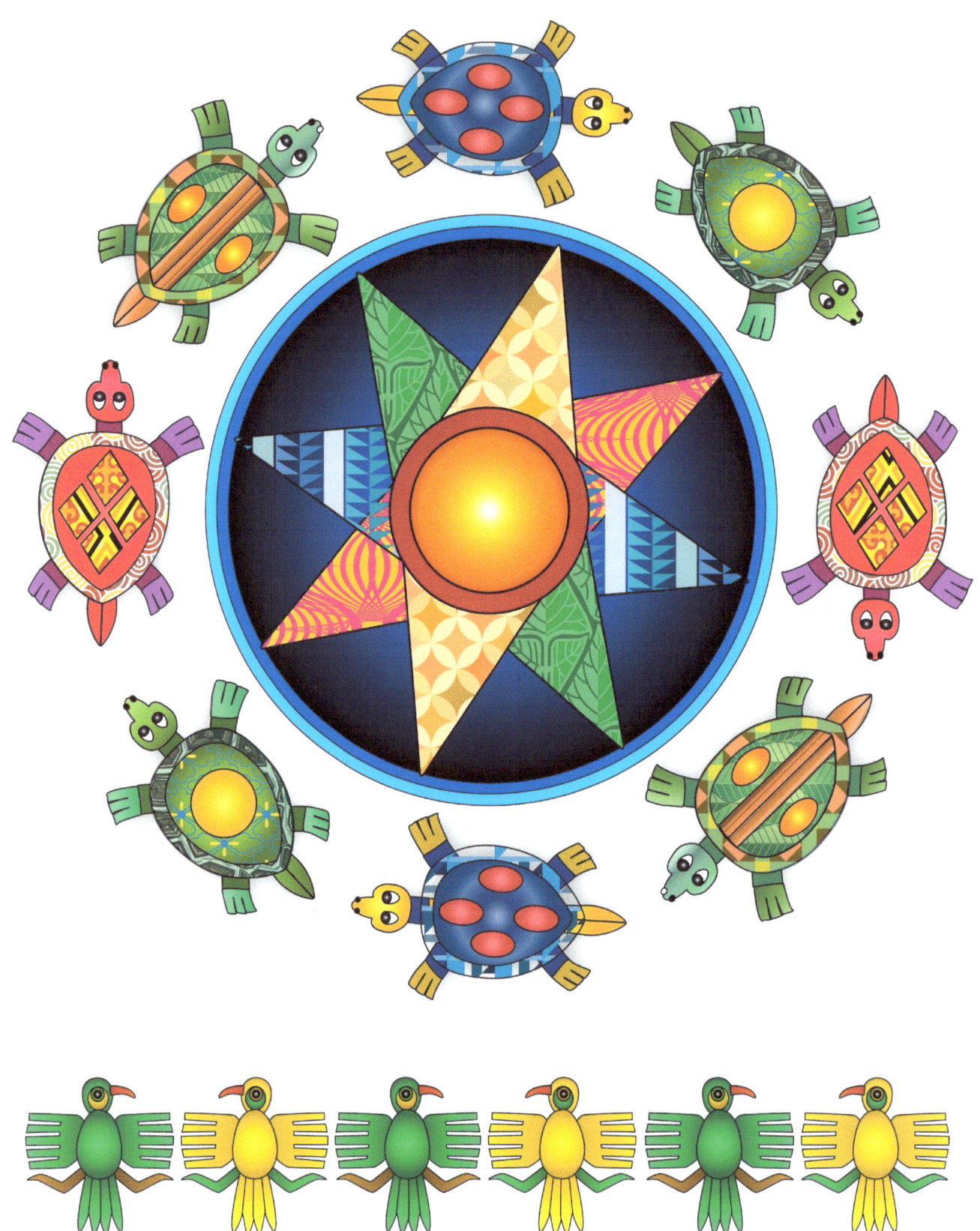

Examples of images created using the elements found in Babylonian Art.

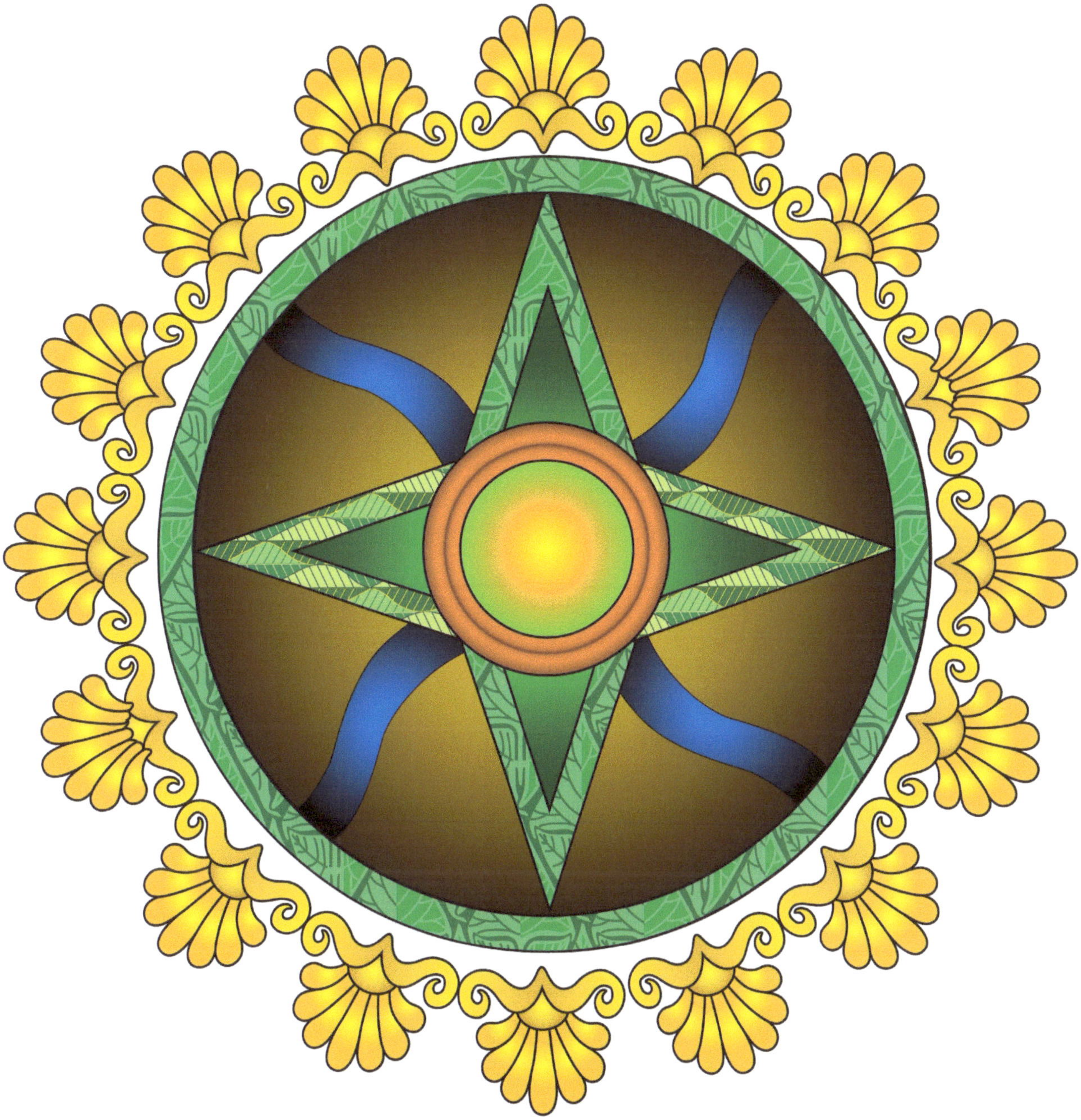

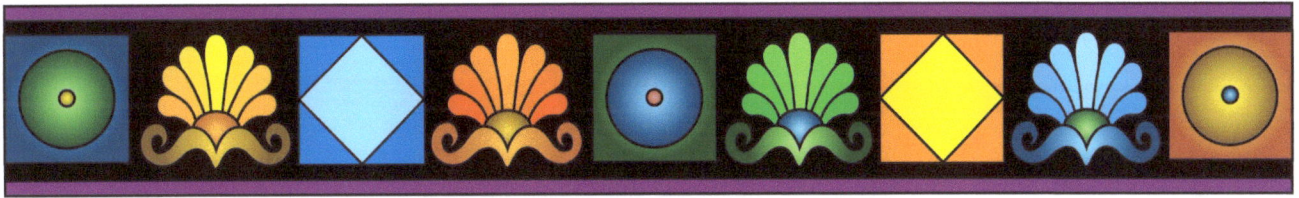

Examples of images created using the elements found in Babylonian Art.

Chinese Art during the early Stone Age consisted of pottery and sculptures, which dates back to as early as 10,000 B.C.E., and is still inarguably one of the oldest tradition of art in the world. It is often classified by the succession of the Chinese emperors, most of which have lasted hundreds of years.

The fundamentals of a Chinese painting consisted of six principals, which were: First, creating a life-like tone and atmosphere; Second, building structures through brushwork; Third, depicting the forms and things as they are; Fourth, applying appropriate coloring; Fifth, composition; and finally the Sixth, which was transcribing and copying.

Traditional ink wash paintings were practiced by scholar-officials. The landscape was developed as aesthetic values dependent on the imagination of the artist. Artists painted human figures from the Han period (206 B.C.E. - 221 C.E.) to the Tang Dynasties (618 C.E. - 907 C.E.). They preserved paintings on silk banners, lacquered objects, and even on tomb walls. From the Five Dynasties to the Northern Song era (960 C.E. - 1127 C.E.) is known as, 'The Golden age of Chinese Landscapes.'

Decorative art is vital among the traditional Chinese art. Over the years, countless fine works produced in various imperial factories by Chinese artists in the form of porcelain, textile and so forth. Chinese ceramic ware was continuously developed since the predynastic periods as a significant form of Chinese art. Chinese jade was attributed with magical powers and was used both in the Stone and Bronze ages for large weapons, tools, and vessels.

Like paintings, calligraphy was also deeply appreciated in China. Chinese amateurs, aristocrats, and scholar-officials made the time to perfect the technique and gain the necessary sensibility for calligraphic brushwork. Calligraphy was thought to be the highest and purest form of painting. Wang Xizhe was a famous Chinese Calligrapher and lived in the 4th Century B.C.E.

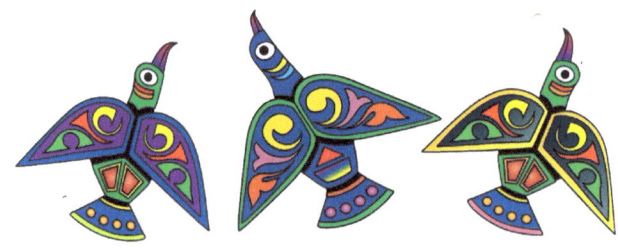

= a synopsis of =
Babylonian Art

The earliest politico-religious and artistic expressions of man within a mature culture were found in the region known today as the ancient Middle East. The civilization stretches from Egypt and Anatolia in the West to the Iranian plateau in the East and beyond. The Babylonian Civilization was a natural offspring of the Sumerian Civilization. Babylon means "The Gate of Gods," and was the administrative capital when the Ur dominated the central and the southern Mesopotamian Civilization.

A double, four-sided wall five miles long, flanked by a canal used as a moat defended the city. The system of cuneiform writing on clay and seals originated there in 3100 B.C. This writing system was adopted in other neighboring countries.

Babylon became the spiritual and temporal capital of the region during the reign of King Hammurabi (1792 - 1750 B.C.E.). There are bas-relief sculptures showing King Hammurabi accepts the text of laws from the God Shamash, a patron of justice. King Hammurabi is also represented in sculptures, kneeling in prayer. The main gate was decorated with figures of dragons, the emblem of the God Marduk, and the bulls, associated with Adad, the God of storms with enameled bricks. Terracotta reliefs that were discovered are elegant and dates back to the early 2000 B.C.E. The terracotta sculptures and carpentry depict the daily life of the Babylonians.

After King Hammurabi's death, Mesopotamia was torn for centuries by foreign invaders, who razed the city of Babylon. In 612 B.C.E., under the rule of King Nebuchadnezzar II, Babylonia developed to perfection creating the most striking artworks with their relief molded polychrome glazed brick walls. It contains up to 575 reliefs of lions, dragons, and bulls of all created with incredible craftsmanship.

In the king's palace, the Ishtar Gate, and the royal processional road, made Babylonia a city of splendor and unrivaled magnificence. Skilled artisans drew upon materials and styles from an area bounded by Egypt in the west all the way to India in the east. Unfortunately, the new splendor was short lived, as Babylonia fell with more invasions and eventually crumbled.

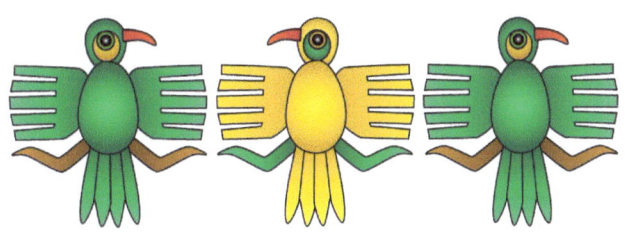

OTHER TITLES IN THIS SERIES

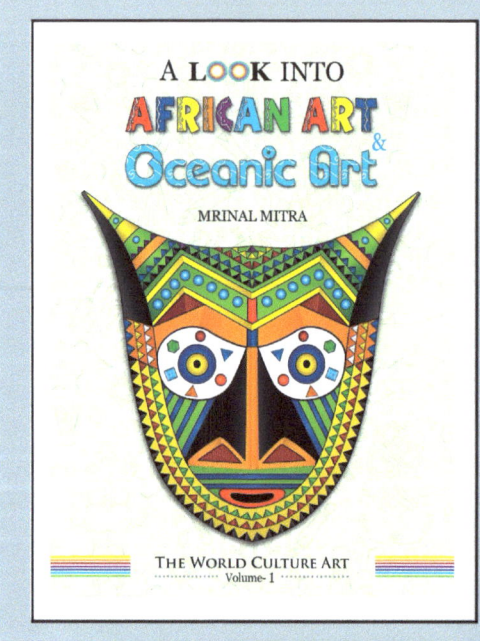

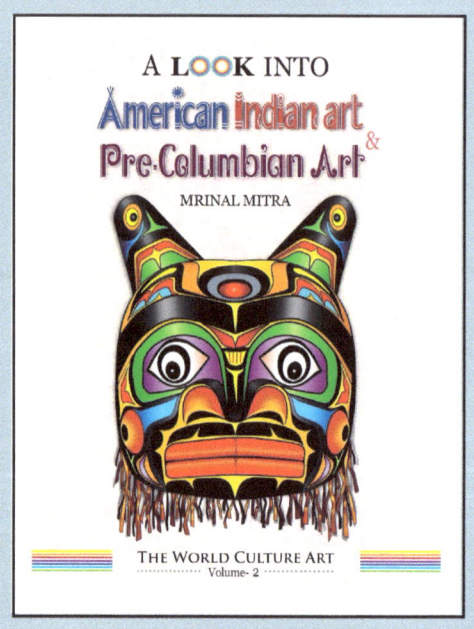

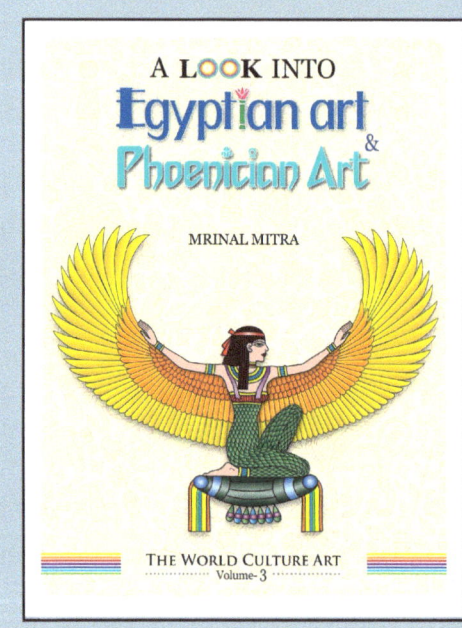

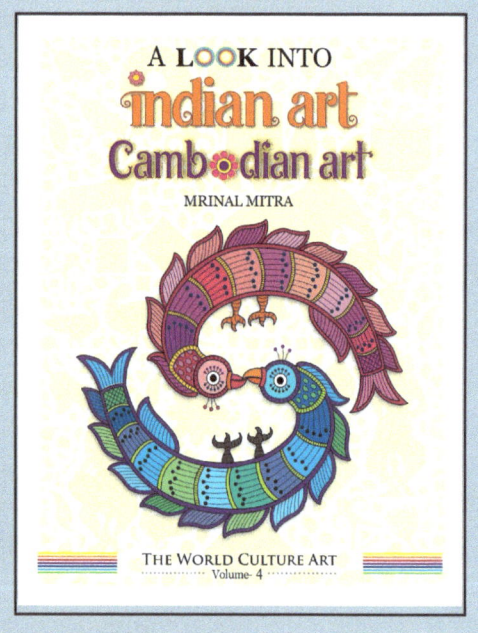

About the Author

Mrinal Mitra has earned a number of prestigious awards, both Indian and International, and received honors for his outstanding illustrations. Some of his recognitions include; The Noma Concours Award (twice), Tokyo, Japan, Illustrators Award, and Children`s Choice Award, India, and Honors from German Television `Transtel`, BRNO- CSSR, and UNICEF, New York, USA.

Many of his talented artworks have been exhibited in various countries such as; India, Japan, Italy, Czech Republic, Iran, and New Zealand. Mitra has authored, designed, and illustrated trades and educational children books for many Indian as well as Multinational Book Publishers around the globe.

Printed by CreateSpace, an Amazom.com company.
Available from Amazon.com, CreateSpace.com, and other retail outlets.

www.ingramcontent.com/pod-product-compliance
Lightning Source LLC
Chambersburg PA
CBHW051107180526
45172CB00002B/814